Please return or renew by
latest date below

LOANS MAY BE RENEWED BY PHONE
648-5710

Ro a C.
Economic
Prospects

Information Centre

Royale sur l'union
économique et les perspectives d
développement du Canada

Centre d'information

Profitability and unemployment

Profitability and unemployment

Based on the Marshall Lectures
given at the University of Cambridge 1978

Edmond Malinvaud

Cambridge University Press

Cambridge

London   New York   New Rochelle   Melbourne   Sydney

& Editions de la Maison des Sciences de
l'Homme

Paris

Published by the Press Syndicate of the University of Cambridge
The Pitt Building, Trumpington Street, Cambridge CB2 1RP
32 East 57th Street, New York, NY 10022, USA
296 Beaconsfield Parade, Middle Park, Melbourne 3206, Australia
and Editions de la Maison des Sciences de l'Homme
54 Boulevard Raspail, 75270 Paris Cedex 06

First published 1980

Printed and bound in Great Britain
at The Pitman Press, Bath

Library of Congress Cataloguing in Publication Data

Malinvaud, Edmond.

Profitability and unemployment.

Includes index.

1. Unemployed. 2. Profit. 3. Economic policy.
I. Title.
HD5706.M154   339.5   79-21472
ISBN 0 521 22999 5

Contents

Preface

We economists live in very interesting times. Indeed, we have
already witnessed and will witness still more in the coming
years a rethinking of some of our main economic theories. For
such a rethinking two prerequisites are necessary and seem
now to be met: the realization that existing theories are
deficient in important respects and the discovery of new
avenues of approach to the phenomena whose analysis is
deficient.

That our present economic theories still are deficient, needs
no elaboration. Everyone knows that we lack a general,
rigorous and useful framework for taking into account the
actual forms of competition when we consider the determination of prices or resource allocation. Everyone knows
that we lack reliable theoretical tools for studying strategies of
economic and social development. Everyone knows that our
present theories are not very helpful for curing stagflation.

In this book, which grew out of the two Marshall lectures I
gave at the University of Cambridge in April 1978, I shall try
to face a particular challenge, namely to clarify the
relationship between profitability and unemployment. Some
degree of profitability seems to be required if business
stagnation and unemployment are to be avoided; moreover
unemployment affects profitability; but profitability can also
be increased or decreased by economic policies. To grasp this
relationship is particularly important at present for anyone
working in applied macroeconomics, at least in Western
Europe.

My contention is that our understanding of the matter may be improved by the new theoretical approach of general equilibrium under rigid prices and quantity constraints if this approach is extended to the study of the dynamic process through which prices are revised and equilibrium shifts. In this sense, this book is a companion to my *Theory of Unemployment Reconsidered*.[1]

A general treatment of a dynamic theory, in which, moreover, investment plays an essential role, is beyond my power. Hence, I make a number of simplifying assumptions and in some cases use numerical simulations in place of theorems. Like my previous book, this one will be found to rely on a very particular specification. But I shall have achieved my purpose if I succeed in throwing light on an important aspect of the actual phenomena.

[1] Basil Blackwell, Oxford, 1977.

1 A broad view of the problem

Concern for the relationship between profitability and unemployment reveals much about the present situation of macroeconomic theory. On the one hand, a new approach has appeared in the work of teams studying government policy. Theoreticians should feel uneasy in realizing that this practice was started without their assistance, but they may be sure to learn from examining it and finding out the conditions under which it is valid. On the other hand, the purely abstract reflexion on the foundations of Keynes' *General Theory*, work which has been going on now for more than ten years, is beginning to produce results and to provide the basis for a renewed theoretical system that will be suited to the discussion of a larger spectrum of phenomena. Hence, a reconstruction of the abstract theories of macroeconomic policies is both needed and feasible.

Before a modest attempt at contributing to this reconstruction is discussed, a consideration of its broader context may be useful. This must start with a brief review of the current debates about macroeconomic policies, continue with some methodological notes on the types of approach that are likely to be helpful, and end with a reconsideration of the old question of capital accumulation, income distribution and growth.

The macroeconomic policies under challenge

By a macroeconomic policy we mean a policy that has been

conceived as acting systematically on types of instrument defined in global terms: to raise public expenditures, to curb wage increases, and the like. Such policies are distinct from structural policies, which are directly conceived in more microeconomic terms, as acting for instance on a particular kind of public expenditure or on the wage rate of a particular category of employee. But we do not restrict the scope of macroeconomic policies simply to aggregate demand management. Prices and incomes policies, as are now being used in many countries, are definitely macroeconomic.

When reviewing our analysis of macroeconomic policies, we must successively consider various viewpoints. Let us first consider what the policy makers have to say, second the applied econometricians, third the theoretical economists.

The viewpoint of policy makers

We must realize that, during the past thirty years, and more particularly so during the last decade, significant changes have taken place in the implicit models used by those deciding the main lines of economic policy or those advising on this policy.

In the postwar years and up to the beginning of the sixties, the conventional wisdom was for a very simple form of so-called Keynesian policy. One had to regulate aggregate demand in such a way as to match, as exactly as possible, potential output. The main problem was then to make the tools for such an accurate demand management: the statistics and national accounts required for a correct evaluation of current trends, the institutional set-up for flexible fiscal and monetary policies.

It was then realized that bringing actual output close to potential output was likely to stimulate inflationary pressures, so that at low levels of unemployment a trade-off existed between price stability and full employment. Such a trade-off was made explicit by the famous Phillips curve. Most governments and their advisers then accepted some low rate of inflation as a socially quite admissible price to pay for high employment and fast growth.

But from the middle of the sixties on, more and more people felt that this conventional wisdom accepted too optimistic a view of the working of our economic system. More precisely, that the simple demand management rule is quite correct in the short run, but that permanent reliance on it as the unique tool of macroeconomic policy may lead to increasing financial disequilibria in the long run. The discussion about the Phillips curve well illustrates the difficulty: the rate of inflation that has to be accepted in order to achieve a given level of employment is defined in comparison with the rate of anticipated inflation and the latter of course adapts to recently experienced inflation; hence a policy aiming at a permanently low unemployment rate is bound to lead to a permanently accelerating rate of inflation. In other words, if the short-term consequences of demand management are undoubtedly favourable, its medium-term consequences may, under some circumstances, be socially or economically unacceptable.

In this phase, renewed interest was given to incomes policies as a useful complement to demand management policies: since the accelerating rate of inflation was due to market and social forces that pushed up nominal wages and other rates of remuneration too quickly, a deliberate policy of wage restraint, preferably supported by price controls and by a system of observation of all incomes, was advocated. In France, for instance, the need for such a policy had already been argued for in 1964 by the well-known economist Pierre Massé, then Commissaire du Plan.

Not only did we have inflation, but we could also observe in the early seventies in some countries a declining trend in rates of profit. And rates of profit went down sharply everywhere in the Western world when the price of oil was raised. Considering the prevailing low profitability in business and the high uncertainty that surrounded future growth, advisers of governments were very concerned about the investment shortage that would result; they feared that such a shortage would reinforce the trend toward mounting unemployment, a trend that was already only too visible. The best expression of this new concern was given by Helmut Schmidt, the head of the social democrat government of Western Germany: 'The profits of today are the investments of tomorrow and the investments of tomorrow make the employment of the day after tomorrow.' From then on, the analysis of macroeconomic policy stressed equally two aspects of the prevailing situation and of its foreseeable evolution: aggregate demand on the one hand, profitability on the other hand.

In short, experience with macroeconomic policies leads us to introduce now two new dimensions into our current analysis. We should study not only the immediate consequences of contemplated measures but also their medium-term consequences. We should consider profitability as well as aggregate demand.

The new concern for profitability as a prerequisite for growth takes us back to a type of analysis that was done in the thirties. To take just one example, Nicolas Kaldor recently drew attention to a very interesting lecture[1] given by the German economist, Hans Joachin Rüstow, who explained the kind of analysis that he used when he was advising Brüning's government in 1928–31. Reading this lecture one cannot help being impressed by the many similarities with what is being now done.

This change in the macroeconomic analysis used by policy makers recently occurred without the assistance of theoretical economists. It was a reaction to the economic problems faced by governments. Whether and under what conditions the new analysis is well founded has not yet been carefully explored. Today it is a real challenge to theoreticians, who should carefully scrutinize this question. When studying the role of

[1] 'The origins of the economic crisis towards the end of the Weimar republic and how it was overcome – A comparison with the present recession', H.-J. Rüstow, Theodor Heuss Academy, 18 September 1977.

profitability on employment, theorists should not of course look for arguments that permit them to advocate the present analysis of policy makers, but should rather examine when, if ever, and under what conditions, this analysis is correct and appropriate.

The contribution of applied econometricians

A theoretician has mixed feelings when he wonders what he can learn from econometric models which are intended to make the preparation of macroeconomic policy more objective. On the one hand these models are part of the body of knowledge of economic phenomena, since, starting from specifications that relied on the prevailing conceptions of these phenomena, they have been fitted to statistical series and revised in the light of experience accumulated throughout the world during the past two decades. A theoretical economist who neglected econometric models would be much like a theoretical physicist who ignored what was happening in laboratory experimentation.

On the other hand, neither is the performance of these models impressive, nor is the representation they give of economic phenomena easily interpretable. I do not need to dwell here on the performance. Suffice it to say that econometric models do not provide the accurate picture that their presentation often suggests. We must recognize, however, first that they provide a most useful tool for policy makers who would otherwise often succumb to the temptation of relying on their subjective intuition, and second that the forecasts they produce compare favourably with those based on less analytical methods, and especially favourably when economic evolution is suffering from strong disturbances, as at present.

But for theoretical purposes the lesson to be learned from econometric models is not easily drawn. Even when they refer to a single economy, they differ among themselves in their specification, and the differences often are essential, without any one model clearly dominating its main competitors. In a recent address to the Econometric Society[2] Christopher Sims starts from the complaint that econometric models are not 'the arena within which macroeconomic theories confront reality and thereby confront each other'; he then goes on to explain why this is so and to present his views as to how the present situation should be improved. While his positive recommendations may raise some reservations, one must recognize that his concern is quite relevant.

This unsatisfactory situation should not, however, be seen as a complete excuse. Theoreticians must now try to see the present work of applied econometricians in perspective and to elucidate how it relates to the present rethinking of macroeconomic policies.

In one respect one finds a clear confirmation of the conclusions drawn from the viewpoint of policy makers: a good grasp of macroeconomic phenomena requires a dynamic specification with many distributed lags; hence, the immediate consequences of exogenous changes must be distinguished from their medium-term consequences and often are significantly different. The trend in applied econometric research during the last decade has been toward taking into better account the various distributed lags, even though this makes the building, estimation and use of models much more difficult. The need to look beyond the immediate consequences of policy changes has been well understood by users of econometric models, who now often work on the definition of appropriate strategies for economic policy and are even adapting the techniques of optimal control for their needs.

One should recognize that the dynamics of the whole system are always complex and vary uncomfortably from one econometric model to another, even when each is intended to describe the same reality. Hence, long-term consequences of economic policies remain obscure. But at least one knows that

[2] C. A. Sims, 'Macroeconomics and Reality', 1977 Fisher–Schultz lecture, Vienna; University of Minnesota discussion paper.

short-term impact multipliers may be misleading.

Does one also find confirmation of the proposition that the study of aggregate demand should be supplemented by the study of profitability, of its determinants and of its impact on economic activity? The answer is not a definitive yes, we must admit.

Since the main inspiration of model builders was the type of Keynesian theory that became popular in the fifties, one should not be surprised to find that the formation of aggregate demand has a central place in present econometric models. But one should also note that these models have never been limited to a single 'block' representing aggregate demand and that the trend has been in developing mainly other blocks. In particular the determination of changes in prices and wages also plays a central role now in all models. Pressure on capacity is recognized as a determining factor both in the investment equation and in the price–wage equations. A high pressure on capacity is of course correlated with high prices and with high profits. Realized profits, considered as providing liquidity, are usually present on the right-hand side of the investment equation; they and other variables may act as proxies for profitability. But a more direct measure of the latter concept should be introduced both in the demand for investment and in the demand for labour functions so as to test the present conceptions of policy makers. More will be said about that in the next chapter.

The monetarist standpoint

Since the final outcome of the present inquiry should be to help in defining economic policies, we must of course make reference to a debate that directly concerns macroeconomic policies and has been given considerable publicity outside the economics profession, namely the debate between so-called monetarists and so-called Keynesians.

As economists we should not be proud of the way in which

this debate started, developed and was conveyed to the public, because the main issues were not clearly stated and appropriately discussed. As was explained by Franco Modigliani,[3] the question is not whether money matters and whether the money supply should be controlled. It is rather to know what role should be assigned to stabilization policies. Keynesians believe that modern economies need to be stabilized. In contrast monetarists hold that there is no serious need for stabilization and that in any case, when governments and their advisers claim to stabilize, they are more likely by their interventions to increase than to decrease the instability of the economy. Hence, monetarists have often given the very simple prescription that the government should not use budgetary policy and that the money supply should increase at a constant rate, chosen so as to permit long-term financial orthodoxy, no consideration being paid to a detailed analysis of what the current situation may be.

We must recognize that the monetarist criticism is well taken when it points to the fact that Keynesian stabilization policies are less powerful than was thought fifteen years ago: their short-term impacts are smaller, their medium-term impacts sometimes perverse. Appropriate macroeconomic policies are more difficult to conceive than is granted in the now traditional textbook teaching. It may even be that, in some countries and during the rather calm period of the fifties and sixties, macroeconomic policies were, on the whole, destabilizing; but, first, even this has not been demonstrated; second, it cannot be true for all countries (France in particular); third, economists should learn from their mistakes rather than giving up hopes of improvement.

One must also grant to the monetarists that present conceptions of the dynamics of economic phenomena still leave a number of large loopholes. Such loopholes are particularly noteworthy in the interaction of short-term

[3] F. Modigliani, 'The Monetarist Controversy or, Should We Forsake Stabilization Policies?', *American Economic Review*, March 1977.

fluctuations and long-term trends. The formation of expectations then plays an important role; indeed, expectations cannot be taken as independent of the stabilization strategy chosen by public authorities, particularly so when the strategy is consistently followed over a long period. If no credibility attaches to the extreme form of the 'rational expectations hypothesis', according to which individual behaviour compensates for and nullifies whatever policy measures are adopted, a correct evaluation of the impact of such measures must account for induced changes in expectations. But no compelling reason exists for the belief that economic research, both theoretical and econometric, is unable to discover more and more completely what these induced changes are likely to be.

To sum up, let us remember that the study of macro-economic policies now faces a number of challenges and let us then find in this situation reasons for giving it priority rather than for neglecting it.

The position of a new theoretical approach

To discuss the role that the relationship between profitability and unemployment should play in the study of macroeconomic policies we must use theoretical models that can trace medium-term consequences; indeed, the fluctuations of investment are at the centre of the phenomenon. These models must moreover recognize that 'disequilibrium' is a major feature to be taken into account: not only does unemployment reveal an imbalance in quantities, but high or low profitability reveals an imbalance in prices as well.

Medium-term evolutions[4] are the subject matter of theories of business fluctuations and indeed a reconsideration of these

[4] We shall speak here of short, medium and long term without presenting any general definition in abstract terms for these words. They are intended to mean respectively something like: 'a few months', 'two to six years', 'fifteen years and more'. The respective appropriate theories are taken to be those of temporary equilibrium, business fluctuations, economic growth.

theories is needed. Few of them have resisted the test of time. The accelerator–multiplier model and its various elaborations remain practically the only ones present in economists' minds. Teaching on business fluctuations starts with them and quickly goes on to consider econometric models rather than economic theories.

The main additions to the accelerator–multiplier type of models should be the representation of prices and of income distribution, of the endogenous changes that they experience in booms and depressions, and finally of the feedback they have on capital accumulation. That such additions should be made has, of course, been well understood for a long time by all experts in this field. But the subject seems to have been rather neglected recently by theoreticians.

The accelerator–multiplier model may be described as a fully fixed price dynamic theory. Not only are prices rigid in the short run while a 'temporary equilibrium' is being established, but they also remain unchanged from one period to the next one, from one temporary equilibrium to the following one. The dynamic process concerns only quantities, so that prices and income distribution do not even have to be represented.

A less restrictive dynamic theory is needed, in which prices will be allowed to shift from one temporary equilibrium to the next one. The shifts will of course depend on the excess demands or supplies that occur in the various markets at the current equilibrium. It is precisely such an attempt at theoretical construction that must concern us here.[5]

Let it be said, to avoid misunderstandings at this stage, that the purpose is not to exhibit and explain cycles in business

[5] The model to be developed here has a formal characteristic that can also be found in some of those elaborated by the theory of business fluctuations, namely, it contains several 'regimes' and it views the economic evolution as shifting at times from one regime to another. But each one of its regimes will be based on a complete economic analysis and will claim to represent, although in a very simplified manner, a type of situation that can be observed for a more or less prolonged period.

activity. Indeed, the dynamic evolutions to be considered will only have weak cyclical components, if any. The purpose is rather to determine models that will be helpful for our reflexion on medium-term economic evolutions. We now know from the econometric work of the last few decades that cyclicity as such is not a dominant feature of the phenomena to be explained.

The contemplated theoretical effort should probably not overlook that there might be something to be learnt from mathematical growth theories. These are certainly not immediately appropriate in the present context. Existing mathematical growth models take essentially no account of the lags in investment and in the adaptation of expectations. Moreover, whereas they do consider sequences of temporary equilibria, they assume that all markets are cleared in each equilibrium and therefore that prices are fully flexible. These features are easily explained because growth theories were developed with long-term questions in view rather than medium-term ones. But these features are at variance with those needed in the present case.

However, some growth models and their balanced growth paths should be introduced within any fully satisfactory theory of medium-term evolution. The risk exists that the specifications chosen in a medium-term theory have inadmissible long-term implications that do not appear unless the associated growth models are studied. Moreover, the lessons to be learned from a description of theoretical medium-term evolutions are made clearer if these evolutions are seen against the background of balanced long-term paths.

The time dimension is, of course, essential when the question is raised as to what the appropriate hypotheses to make about price and quantity adjustments are. These adjustments depend not only on the degrees of imbalance experienced in different parts of the economy, but also on technological constraints, on the forms of competition, on implicit or explicit long-term institutional arrangements and so on. A detailed representation is impossible in any macroeconomic theory and a short-cut must be found that will give a simple image of the result of all these factors; but the appropriate image will of course not be the same in theories that are intended to look at the same reality from different angles.

For most growth theories one can accept a model in which adjustments are taken to be instantaneous and imbalance is neglected, because the time dimension is long. For macroeconomic theories of short-term equilibrium it has been argued extensively that prices and wages may be taken as fixed (but interest rates as fully flexible) in a first approximation, while quantities bear the burden of adjustment to decisions that otherwise would be mutually incompatible. It has been convincingly argued that such a hypothesis would not be realistic if imbalance in some markets were large, because price competition would then be effective even in the short run.[6] When disequilibrium in a market should be taken as large in this respect is of course to some extent a matter of judgment. But the main conclusion to be drawn is that the new theories of short-term fixed price equilibrium are intended to apply in conditions under which excess demands or supplies are rather small. We may say that they are intended to apply in the neighbourhood of a Walrasian equilibrium.

Indeed, the same remark should be made about the present study. The medium-term evolutions to be considered will be assumed to take place not too far from the Walrasian growth path that would obtain if no lags occurred in the adjustment of prices as well as quantities.

The theory of medium-term evolution will therefore start from the now familiar view of short-term equilibrium but supplement it in two ways: by proposing a description of the induced changes in prices and wages, but also by considering explicitly quantities that are rigid in the short run but flexible in the long run; whereas production and consumption

[6] See A. Coddington's review of *The Theory of Unemployment Reconsidered* in *Journal of Economic Literature*, September 1978.

are determined by the conditions of the current equilibrium, the building up of productive capacity and the substitution of capital for labour play an important role as adjustment factors.[7]

The question might be raised as to whether the same time dimension is involved for the revision of prices and wages as for capital accumulation. The classical teaching of micro-economic theories may lead most economists to react to this question with the answer that price and wage adjustments are definitely faster. But consideration of actual data shows that, except for exogenous shocks, time is required for the major macroeconomic shifts concerning the rate of inflation, the rate of increase of real wages or the rate of profit; this time may be counted in years, which is also the proper unit for following fluctuations of capital accumulation.

These methodological notes stress the fact that capital accumulation and income distribution will play a central role in any attempt at explaining medium-term evolution. This is of course particularly true if the role of profitability must be clarified. Before any formalization is introduced, a heuristic and literal examination of the main phenomena to be tackled in this respect will be useful.

Capital accumulation, income distribution and growth

Smooth medium-term growth requires an appropriate rate of accumulation of fixed capital, by which is meant two things: first, the growth of productive capacity should match the growth of full employment demand in such a way that there is

[7] Attempts at making the theory of fixed price equilibria dynamic have recently been undertaken. The accumulation of consumers wealth when prices and wages are kept fixed is studied by V. Böhm in 'Disequilibrium dynamics in a simple macroeconomic model', *Journal of Economic Theory*, 1978, pp. 179–99. Progressive adaptation of prices and wages is moreover introduced by S. Honkapohja in 'On the dynamics of disequilibria in a macro model with flexible wages and prices', see M. Aoki and A. Marzollo, ed., *New Trends in Dynamic System Theory and Economics*, proceedings of the Udine conference, Academic Press, 1979.

neither shortage nor real excess of capacity over full employment demand; second, existing capacity must be such that its full use implies a demand for labour just equal to the available labour force. An appropriate rate of accumulation of fixed capital in turn requires an appropriate income distribution, that will both generate the proper savings and sustain the corresponding investment demand. Hence, making progress in our understanding of medium-term evolution depends on our ability to grasp better the medium-term dynamics of income distribution, certainly one of the most difficult questions, if not *the* most difficult question, of economic theory. Let us consider these various points a little more closely.

An appropriate rate of accumulation of fixed capital

Should we accept the notion that at each time an appropriate stock of capital could be defined, a stock that will, of course, usually differ from the existing one? We certainly should if reality is to conform to the aggregate Harrod–Domar model with a fixed capital–output ratio and a fixed labour–output ratio. Output Y, capital K and labour L would have to be three proportional numbers. Hence, K would have to match both aggregate demand Y and available labour force L. Even if we admit that somehow Y adjusts so as to be in the right proportion to L, a strict condition is imposed on K.

Reality is not that simple. We have learned, from Joan Robinson in particular, that defining aggregate capital K implies still stronger conventions than those already necessary for the definition of aggregate output Y and aggregate labour L. But we may still consider the Harrod–Domar model as a simple image for a microeconomic reality in which each particular worker is available only to produce one particular output, and for this needs a well specified set of capital equipment. The evolution of the stock of capital would then have to adjust to what the evolution of the labour force is going to be, and incidentally the composition of the demand for goods would also need to grow in conformity with it.

There is no doubt that many of our fellow citizens see the problem of full employment growth in this simple way. They cannot be completely right because they then forget the implications for the evolution of consumption. Mobility of labour between production processes does exist and taking advantage of it is one important source of economic growth. However, the public concern has a strong appeal and we should keep it in mind. It may give some justification for the model to be used in the next chapter, in which a Harrod–Domar technology will be directly assumed. For the time being let us consider against this background the more sophisticated models that have been developed in modern economic theory.

These models all stress the association between technical progress and the building of new equipment; hence, any piece of equipment must be characterized in particular by the date at which it was built. The models differ, however, in the range of technological choice that they recognize, on the one hand for the use of a historically given stock of equipment, on the other hand for the materialization into new equipment of a given investment effort. The technology is said to be 'clay–clay' if the labour and capital inputs are taken to be strict complements in both cases. It is said to be 'putty–clay' if some substitutability exists when the building of new equipment is decided, but not when old equipment is used. Finally a 'putty–putty' technology assumes substitutability on existing equipment as well.

Speaking of the productive capacity and of the labour requirement of a given stock of equipment, as will be done in the next chapter, is to assume away all possibility of choice in the productive use of this stock, and hence to assume away any influence of prices and remuneration rates on the supply of output, and on the demand of labour corresponding to this supply. But some economists have shown that, even with the clay–clay or putty–clay technology, this influence exists to the extent that the price system determines whether and up to what age it is profitable to use older equipment. Neglecting this fact[8] we shall be likely to underestimate the role of the price system in determining output and employment. This is why we shall take up the question again briefly in the last chapter.

At present we must recognize that the notion of an 'appropriate stock of fixed capital' cannot be made precise by looking only at the physical conditions of production: the technology and the labour force. It is interdependent with other aspects of the current situation; or if we speak in theoretical terms, it is interdependent with other aspects of the temporary equilibrium. We may even go so far as to say that, neglecting some unrealistic specifications, a price system could always be found that would make the existing stock of capital appear appropriate: the real wage rate will simply have to be low enough if the existing stock is small and high enough if it is large. In other words, only when we limit in some way the range of feasible price systems, can we conclude that the existing stock is inappropriate.

Considering now not the stock of capital but its rate of increase, the rate of accumulation of capital, we realize that it will depend on the expectations that firms entertain not only of the demand for their output but also of the prices and remuneration rates that will prevail. This conclusion is of course reinforced when we take into account the range of choices that exist, except in the clay–clay technology, for the type of equipment to be built. Moreover, expectations about the price system are related to the past and present price systems.

Accepting full price and wage flexibility we might claim

[8] Strictly speaking, we should say that, with the Harrod–Domar technology, the price system determines whether firms will wish to produce at full capacity or to produce nothing. But the latter possibility would only appear for prices and remuneration rates that are quite unlikely to be observed, since they would imply a negative *gross* income for firms.

that the notion of an appropriate rate of capital accumulation does not make more sense than the notion of an appropriate stock of capital. Starting from any present stock and level of investment, there will be a feasible full employment growth path that could originate from them and be sustained at least in the medium run;[9] this requirement would only imply that appropriate levels and future time paths be found for the various prices and remuneration rates.

But since prices and wages are not fully flexible, since for instance deviations of the course of the real wage rate from its feasible long-term trend are difficult to implement and socially harmful, we should aim at a *rate of capital accumulation that makes possible a full employment growth path that would not need prices and remuneration rates to deviate from their feasible long-term trends*. Such a rate of capital accumulation may rightly be qualified as appropriate.

An appropriate income distribution

When we speak of the feasible long-term trends of prices and remuneration rates, we seem to imply that these are predetermined, which is of course not the case. Finding out these trends must be simultaneous with finding out the appropriate rate of capital accumulation. But at the present stage, at which several aspects of the problem are only just being explored, this simultaneity may be neglected. With this remark in mind, let us now turn to considering what is such a sustainable price system, or, equivalently, what is an appropriate income distribution.

The income distribution must be such as to generate the appropriate savings. We know from Harrod, Domar and Kaldor that this requirement is strong in the aggregate model

---

[9] We know, from the work of Frank Hahn in particular, that difficulties are conceivable in the long run in models with several capital goods and that such full employment growth with complete price flexibility might be unstable.

with full complementarity between labour and capital.[10] When substitutability between the two main inputs is recognized, the requirement is less strict since future growth may be more or less capital intensive.

The relation between the income distribution and savings should, of course, take real wealth effects into account. In an analysis of long-term trends these effects cannot be negligible since savings means accumulation of wealth. The importance of real wealth considerations is sometimes played down; but it should play a central part in any theory that claims to explain the long-term income distribution from savings requirement.

In any case saving is the easy side of the issue, since the income distribution must also be such as to sustain the appropriate investment. Indeed, the relation between income distribution and the corresponding medium-term level of the investment that will then be sustained is far from clear.

This relation is clear in the mathematical models in which economic growth is seen to result from a sequence of temporary competitive equilibria with full price flexibility and capital reversibility. But these models assume equilibrium in each period whereas there always is an element of disequilibrium in investment, as we know from Schumpeter in particular and as we argued above. Moreover, they neglect the combination of uncertainty and irreversibility that makes investment so sensitive to business prospects and anticipations. Hence, they assume in effect that the profit resulting from the marginal efficiency of investment can be immediately realized.

We have no reason to discard completely the notion that the marginal efficiency of investment must equal the rate of profit on alternative uses of capital, hence in particular that it must equal the rate of interest. But we must view the efficiency of each investment as being evaluated for the more or less long period during which the corresponding equipment will be used and therefore as being both expected and uncertain. It

[10] N. Kaldor, 'Alternative Theories of Distribution', *Review of Economic Studies*, 1955–1956.

depends on expectations about future prices, wages and interests; it is therefore related to the current values of these variables; roughly speaking we may say that it is higher the higher the current profit rate. But in order for the investment to look profitable and therefore to be undertaken, it seems also to be necessary for the margin over the interest rate to be higher the higher the uncertainty about the future.

Such a formulation is consistent both with the abstract theory of growth, when we modify it in such a way as to take irreversibility and uncertainty into account, and with the new concern of policy makers about profitability. To describe the income distribution of the seventies as inadequate does not seem to contradict theoretical thinking, given that the profit rate had fallen and uncertainty about future growth had increased.

We must, however, recognize that we do not yet have an explicit theory which would give us a fully reliable guide for determining at each moment the appropriate income distribution, given the requirements for future growth. We must rely on econometric models whose results in this respect do not seem to be robust. The results are certainly sensitive to the way in which the uncertainty of expectations is entered into the investment function. But the main difficulty lies in the exogenous forecasts that have to be made about the future trend of labour productivity, or more precisely about the future trend of the so-called 'technical progress' that raises the productivity of the various inputs. If this trend has recently slowed, the appropriate rate of capital accumulation has also decreased and therefore the appropriate rate of profit as well.

Moving toward an appropriate income distribution

Starting from the idea that the existing income distribution may sometimes be inappropriate for future growth, we naturally face the question of whether anything should be done about it and how. Will spontaneous factors bring about a more adequate distribution? If a prices and incomes policy is considered, how should it be chosen knowing that, in any case, prices and remuneration rates will move as a result of changes in costs and of excess demands and supplies?

Econometric studies are our main guide at present when we want to characterize the short-term dynamics of income distribution and to see whether it is consistent with the realization of an appropriate distribution. We certainly fear that the wage equation and the price equation are more unstable than, for instance, the production function, because their microeconomic rationale is more complex and aggregation problems are still more formidable for them. But they do represent what we have learned from carefully scrutinizing the course of wages and prices during various periods and within various countries.

These econometric equations clearly show that wages, prices and therefore also profit rates are sticky, more particularly so in cases of excess supply. Any theory of the dynamics of medium-term economic evolution should therefore build its models by taking full account of this stickiness. This is why the new theories of general equilibrium with fixed prices and rationing provide a good theoretical framework if they are supplemented by properly specified formulations of how wages, prices and rationing change from one period to the next.

When one builds on the results of econometric studies concerning the price and wage equations in order to draw conclusions about the medium-term consequences of economic policies, one must, however, feel somewhat uneasy. Indeed, on the one hand working with econometric equations one soon realizes that the medium-term dynamics of the income distribution are not robust to conceivable changes in the equations, which have been fitted to portray short-term changes at least as much as medium-term ones. On the other hand one may wonder whether there are not economic, or even socio-political, medium-term feedbacks that appear only in cases of prolonged and important deviations from the income distribution that is sustainable in the long run. Indeed, the recent deliberate attempts in many countries at restoring the profit rate could conceivably be viewed as a necessary consequence of preceding developments, a consequence that does not follow from the dynamics applying to more 'normal' times.

But I do not think we can do better today than to use available econometric equations on prices and wages. An alternative, which is not very different, has been suggested, namely to consider directly econometric equations applying to the profit share or to the wage share in national income. My own reading of the experience with this alternative approach is that it performs rather less well than the more common one. Moreover, it does not lend itself easily to being entered into a theory of short-term evolution, in which nominal values must be taken into account.

2 The appropriate income distribution

In order to understand the role of profitability and to study the medium-term consequences of economic policies, we need to build a precise theory of the dynamic working of our economies.

In this book we shall mainly concentrate our attention on a very crude model, from which we shall depart only in the last chapter. This model will be formulated directly in terms of the main aggregates; it will assume in particular a fixed labour supply, no technical progress and strict complementarity between labour and capital. Extreme hypotheses of this type are, of course, not very satisfactory for the problems under consideration; but they make the formal analysis simple, which I take to be sufficient justification at this stage.

The first task in building the model is to set up its variables and behaviour equations, then to study what would in general be long-term balanced growth, but here will be, considering the assumptions made, stationary long-term full employment equilibrium. Such is the aim of this chapter.

Three types of short-term 'equilibrium'

Let L be the (constant) labour force. If it is fully employed it will produce a net output βL, where β is the (constant) productivity of labour, i.e. productivity net of depreciation. But full employment requires two conditions: that there is sufficient aggregate demand and that there is enough capital.

Net aggregate demand for goods will be denoted by d.

Capital, which is given in the short run, as it results from previous investments, will be measured here by its productive capacity $\bar{y}$. We shall suppose that it is always profitable in the short run for firms to produce at full capacity $\bar{y}$ as long as there is sufficient demand and as long as enough labour can be recruited; in other words, the productivity of labour gross of depreciation will always exceed the real cost of labour. This hypothesis, which is not unrealistic for a simple model such as ours, will simplify the following discussion. Net output y will then be given by the minimum of three numbers βL, d and $\bar{y}$: potential output, aggregate demand and productive capacity.[1]

(i) If βL is smaller than the other two numbers, there will be full employment of labour and the demand for labour by firms will be rationed. Simultaneously the demand for goods will also be rationed. We may then speak of a situation of demand *inflation*, or simply 'inflation'.

(ii) If d is smaller than βL and $\bar{y}$, the supply of goods by firms $\bar{y}$ will be rationed and output will be restricted to d. Simultaneously the supply of labour L will also be rationed since employment will only be equal to d/β. This situation of generalized excess supply has now been commonly called for three decades a situation of *Keynesian unemployment*.

(iii) If $\bar{y}$ is smaller than d and βL, the firms will produce at full capacity, but will then not need to recruit the whole labour force and will not be able to fulfil the demand for their output. There will be an excess demand for goods and an excess supply of labour.

---

[1] Such a simple rule for the determination of output follows from the fact that the model is fully aggregated. In actual fact, we may observe that full employment prevails in some industries or regions, whereas productive capacity is binding in some others and demand is lacking in some others still. The consequences of this will be explored in chapter 5. Working with a disaggregated model would be feasible but of course more difficult. I introduced such a model in 'Macroeconomic Rationing of Employment', in J. P. Fitoussi and E. Malinvaud, ed., *Unemployment in Western countries*, Macmillan 1980.

One may argue as to what would be the best description of such a situation. Some people have spoken of 'stagflation' in this respect, but the word is confusing because it is already often used for cases in which one experiences cost inflation with an excess supply of goods. An alternative denomination would be 'Marxian unemployment' to the extent that the existence of a reserve army of workers results from an insufficiently rapid previous capital accumulation; but Marx also refers to the lack of a sufficient demand for goods.

It seems preferable to use an expression that naturally generalizes to cases in which some short-term substitutability between capital and labour remains, namely to cases in which output could be raised by an increase in labour input but in which firms do not find it profitable to recruit more, even when faced by an excess demand for their output. This was the situation that theoretical teaching stressed during the interwar period, when it came from those classical economists against whom Keynes had to argue. Hence, *'classical unemployment'* is a suitable description for a situation in which excess supply of labour and excess demand for goods both prevail.

Besides the three main types of situations there are borderline cases when the minimum of the three numbers βL, d and $\bar{y}$ is reached for at least two of them simultaneously. A particularly interesting case is the one in which:

$$\beta L = d = \bar{y} \tag{1}$$

In this case there is full employment with no excess demand for labour and the supply of goods just clears its own demand. We may speak of a *Walrasian equilibrium*, or perhaps of a 'Marshallian equilibrium', if we want to stress that it is a temporary equilibrium.

To know which situation prevails, one needs to be more specific about economic behaviour and about which adjustments are supposed to take place in the short run. In particular one needs to make it clear which prices and which quantities are supposed to adjust. Here, the extreme hypothesis will be made that the price system is given in the short run and that quantities have to adapt somehow. One should notice, however, that in the present model price flexibility would not suffice to guarantee the realization of a Walrasian equilibrium because here βL and $\bar{y}$ are given in the short run but there is no reason for them to be equal,[2] as required by (1).

Economic flows

Behavioural relations must now be formulated so that a model of short-term equilibrium is defined. But before such relations are specified it is advisable to look at a complete macro-economic representation of the current operations in the simple economy to be studied. Hence, the social accounts will be given and discussed first.

Such a consideration of social accounts is not necessarily required since a model could be directly formulated without this preliminary discussion. But it will be useful not only for reference later, when some specific points will be discussed, but also at this stage for a full understanding of the major simplifications that the model implies.

In the current social accounts in value terms let Y be the output of goods by firms, C be the consumption by households, I be the investment by firms and G be the demand for goods of government.

The equality between resources and uses for the goods (which are fully aggregated and considered as a single commodity) is familiar:

$$Y = C + I + G \qquad (2)$$

The labour income W is paid by firms to households. Other income flows may exist and are then dealt with as transfers;

[2] Of course, one could modify the model to formally permit this equality, for instance by discarding the hypothesis that it is always profitable to produce at full capacity and by introducing a decrease of the labour supply at low real wage rates. But the realization of (1) may still require unrealistically large adjustments of the price system.

Table 1

Current social account

	Uses			Resources		
	Firms	House-holds	Govern-ment	Firms	House-holds	Govern-ment
Product	I	C	G	Y		
Labour	W				W	
Transfers	Z				H	T
Financial assets		$\dot{M}$		$\dot{M}_f$		$\dot{M}_g$

their net effect is a charge Z on firms, with resources H for households and T for government. The accumulation of financial assets by households (the only type of assets they are supposed to hold) is $\dot{M}$; correspondingly the net creation of financial assets is written as $\dot{M}_f$ for firms and $\dot{M}_g$ for government. Equilibrium of economic flows of course requires:

$$Z = H + T \tag{3}$$

$$\dot{M} = \dot{M}_f + \dot{M}_g \tag{4}$$

What type of simultaneous determination of economic flows should be considered? In order to give a first answer to this question, let us say that, in the short-term equilibrium model to be considered, only I, C, G, Y, W and H will appear explicitly. The other flows will be implicitly considered as balancing items or left free to be determined without any feedback to the equilibrium on the goods market. Actually, it is easy to see that, once I, C, G, Y, W and H are known, $\dot{M}$ is determined by the balance of the households' account and only one degree of freedom remains for the simultaneous determination of Z, T, $\dot{M}_f$ and $\dot{M}_g$. The equilibrium is fully determined if, for instance, the value of the net transfers T to government follows from the values of the other flows.

This means in effect that the investment behaviour will not be sensitive to the financial requirement of balancing the firms' accounts: whatever investment I, wage bill W and transfers Z have to be paid, sufficient financial resources $\dot{M}_f$ can be issued to supplement the outcome from production Y. This is of course a simplification that has to be kept in mind. It does not directly bear on the major phenomena that our enquiry is intended to explore, namely the respective roles of aggregate demand and profitability (in particular profitability concerns anticipated profits and not the financial resources brought by realized profits). But the effect of the simplification will have to await consideration till chapter 5.

If household financial savings $\dot{M}$ do not appear in the behaviour equations, it should be noted, however, that the accumulated wealth of households (which will be denoted by M) will be present in the consumption function. Moreover the dynamic process will of course recognize that savings $\dot{M}$ increase accumulated wealth M. On the other hand, firms' behaviour will not depend explicitly on firms' financial liabilities $\dot{M}_f$.

Hypotheses about transfers will also be very crude. They will essentially amount to taking these transfers as exogenous, which will abstract from a number of relationships: realized profits in fact affect transfers through profit taxes and distributed profits; output, consumption and the wage bill are related to taxes; unemployment leads to some relief payments; financial assets and liabilities explain interest payments, and so on. All these relationships are complex; their final effect is not clearcut and cannot be easily introduced in a simple aggregate model. Although they must play a role in applied econometrics, they will be neglected here. This simplification does not seem to imply a systematic bias in the results.

The main variable representing macroeconomic demand management policy will be government consumption G. But transfers H to households will also be considered as exogenous. Although the meaning of the latter hypothesis will never be stressed in the subsequent analysis, it should be interpreted as a subsidiary aspect of budgetary policy.

The consumption and investment functions

We must now specify the behavioural relations. The crucial one for our purpose concerns investment, which is sensitive to both aggregate demand and profitability. Moreover, in our present model with no inventory accumulation and strict complementarity between labour and capital, the investment decision is the only one to be substantially dependent on firms' behaviour (the production decision obeys the very simple and self-evident rule given on p. 23).

Before studying the investment decision, we shall, however, specify the consumption function. This is the only behavioural equation to consider for households, since their labour supply is fixed, while the wage rate and their transfer income are exogenous.

Using lower-case letters to designate real values and P for the price of goods, the consumption decision will determine the volume c of consumption $(C = Pc)$. We shall assume it depends only on real variables and therefore neglect any money illusion. Such an assumption seems to be admissible in a study that concerns medium-term evolutions. The determinants of real consumption will then be:

> the real wage rate w,
> real transfer income h,
> real wealth m,
> the unemployment rate u.

For simplicity's sake we shall suppose that the consumption function is linear with respect to unemployment, which is not very restrictive because we do not want to consider high values of the unemployment rate. The consumption function will then be:

$$c = r(w, h, m) - us(w, h, m) \qquad (5)$$

where r and s are two functions.

The desired productive capacity

When we turn our attention to the investment decision, our purpose cannot be to exhibit a relation that would exactly represent it. As every econometrician knows, this would have to be a very complex relation indeed. Our purpose is rather to find a simple equation that will allow us adequately to formulate a basis for theoretical discussion on the respective roles of profitability and aggregate demand in the study of the short- and medium-term consequences of economic policies.

For the justification of this equation it will be useful to build a preliminary model and permissible to make very strong simplifying assumptions, as long as they are explicitly stated, as long as they will not affect the few essential features of the phenomena and as long as some of their special consequences can be reviewed at the end after a less formal discussion.

First, we shall consider a representative firm and not worry about aggregation difficulties. Second, when formalizing the investment decision of the representative firm, we shall deal with the future during which the new investment will be in operation as if it was a single period. Third, during this period, strict complementarity between labour and capital will apply.

If aggregate demand in the future is d, productivity β, labour supply L, productive capacity $\bar{y}$, then output will be determined as specified on page 23, namely:

$$y = \text{Min}(d, \beta L, \bar{y}) \qquad (6)$$

If the future real wage rate is w, then the current real return from production will be:

$$\left(1 - \frac{w}{\beta}\right) y \qquad (7)$$

At the time of the investment decision some of these variables are unknown, out of the control of the firm and subject to expectations, which may be represented by prior probability distributions. But productive capacity $\bar{y}$ will directly result from present net investment, which in real terms is denoted by i. More precisely, if $1/\gamma$ is the capital–output ratio, future $\bar{y}$ will be equal to present $\bar{y}$ plus γi. In other words deciding on i is equivalent to deciding on future $\bar{y}$; we may therefore in the preliminary model take $\bar{y}$ appearing in (6) as the present decision variable.

The cost of building capacity must be weighed against the expected distribution of returns (7). Except for an inessential constant term reflecting what present capacity is, this cost may be written as $q\bar{y}$. Hence, the net return from production may be written as

$$ R = \left(1 - \frac{w}{\beta} \right) y - q\bar{y} \tag{8} $$

The unit capacity cost q is, of course, a difficult concept, since it has to be defined in such a way as to make $q\bar{y}$ commensurate with (7); but the difficulty is well known from the discussion concerning the now familiar concept of the cost of capital and need not detain the present analysis.

In order to proceed and to study the determination of future $\bar{y}$ for the representative firm, we must make some assumptions about expectations. In conformity with the spirit of the fixed price approach, let us consider the case in which there is certainty over the price variables, but where the quantity variables are out of the control of the firm. This means that in (6) and (8) the variables w, q and β will be taken as exogenous and given, the variables d and L as exogenous but uncertain and the variables y and $\bar{y}$ as endogenous. We shall come back at the end of this section to the justifications for such hypotheses. Suffice it to say at this stage that, when deciding on its future productive capacity, the firm is uncertain as to the future state of demand for its product and perhaps also as to whether it will always be able to recruit the required labour.

It will be convenient to introduce a new exogenous random variable

$$\hat{y} = \text{Min}(d, \beta L) \tag{9}$$

and its cumulative distribution function $F(\hat{y})$; in other words $F(x)$ is the probability that is at present attributed by the firm to the event that in the future $\hat{y} \leqq x$. Let us assume that F has a density function f. Then, since y will be the minimum of $\bar{y}$ and $\hat{y}$, the mathematical expectation[3] of the net return R is:

$$ER = \left(1 - \frac{w}{\beta}\right) \left\{ \int_0^{\bar{y}} v f(v) dv + [1 - F(\bar{y})] \bar{y} \right\} - q\bar{y} \tag{10}$$

The value of $\bar{y}$ that maximizes this expectation must be such that the first derivative of ER with respect to $\bar{y}$ will be equal to zero:

$$\left(1 - \frac{w}{\beta}\right) [1 - F(\bar{y})] - q = 0 \tag{11}$$

and such that its second derivative will be non-positive:

$$w \leqq \beta \tag{12}$$

(assuming $f(\bar{y})$ to be positive).

Equation (11) implicitly determines the capacity $\bar{y}$ to be built as a function of the price variables q, w and of the distribution F representing expectations of the quantity variables. It may be interpreted as meaning that the cost of one extra unit of capacity must be equal to the expected gain resulting from the sale of one extra unit of output multiplied by

[3] This analysis does not take risk aversion into account, since this would complicate the issue without substantially affecting the results from the point of view of this book. If the representative firm is described as maximizing not ER but $EU(R)$, where U is a concave utility function of profits, q in equation (11) must be multiplied by $1 + (1 - w/\beta)A$, where A is a positive number, which increases with absolute risk aversion and typically also increases with the degree of uncertainty.

the probability that the latter could be produced and sold (enough labour and enough demand).

A linear investment function

In order to see what kind of function equation (11) implies for the optimal $\bar{y}$, let us consider how $\bar{y}$ changes as a result of infinitesimal changes δw, δq, δF in the exogenous elements. Differentiation of (11) leads to:

$$(\beta - w) f \delta \bar{y} = -(\beta - w) \delta F - (1 - F) \delta w - \beta \delta q \quad (13)$$

where it is understood that $F, f, \delta F$ are evaluated at $\bar{y}$. Future capacity then appears as a decreasing function of the real wage rate, of the cost of capital and of the probability that $\hat{y}$ be smaller than $\bar{y}$ (taking (12) into account).[4]

It is easy to derive from this an equation for investment i_0 during the present period. If $\bar{y}_0$ denotes existing capacity and $1/\gamma$ the capital–output ratio, one may write:

$$i_0 = \frac{1}{\gamma} (\bar{y} - \bar{y}_0) \quad (14)$$

Hence

$$\delta i_0 = \frac{-\delta F}{f\gamma} - \frac{\delta \bar{y}_0}{\gamma} - \frac{(1 - F) \delta w + \beta \delta q}{(\beta - w) f\gamma} \quad (15)$$

But we still need to say how changes in expectations may be related to changes concerning the present variables so as to derive from (15) a simple behavioural equation for the present period.

---

[4] We shall not discuss precisely here how a change in the degree of uncertainty may affect the optimal capacity level $\bar{y}$. On the one hand, if w, β and q do not change, equation (11) would lead us to think that optimal capacity would tend to *increase* when the degree of uncertainty increases because, in the reference situation, the probability that $\bar{y}$ exceeds the minimum of d and βL is likely to be high. On the other hand, if we take risk aversion into account, an increasing uncertainty is equivalent to an increasing q and therefore to a *decreasing* optimal capacity.

First, since we are working with a model in which no connexion is made between financial assets and transfer incomes, we cannot explicitly introduce interest payments and therefore the cost of capital in any useful way. Second, we may assume that expected changes δw in the future real wage rate are directly related to, and even equal to, present changes δw_0 in this same real rate (lags will be introduced in the next chapter). Third, we may assume that changes in the expectations concerning the variable $\hat{y}$ are similarly related to changes in the present value $\hat{y}_0$ of this variable. More precisely we may accept the simple assumption that, if $\hat{y}_0$ is changed to $\hat{y}_0 + \delta \hat{y}_0$, the probability distribution F is shifted by $\delta \hat{y}_0$. In other words what was $\text{Prob}\{\hat{y} \leq x\}$ becomes $\text{Prob}\{\hat{y} \leq x + \delta \hat{y}_0\}$; hence δF, the variation of $\text{Prob}\{\hat{y} \leq x\}$, is equal to $-f \delta \hat{y}_0$. Looking at (15), we then see that the first two terms may be grouped as:

$$\frac{1}{\gamma} \ (\delta \hat{y}_0 - \delta \bar{y}_0)$$

This said, we come to the simple equation that will be used later to represent investment behaviour, namely:

$$i_0 = a(\beta - e - w_0) + b(\hat{y}_0 - \bar{y}_0) \tag{16}$$

a, b and e being three non-negative parameters (later on we shall come back to the exact timing of the variables). Discussion of this equation can be extended on the basis of the preceding considerations.

Equation (16) is deliberately simple. In particular, it is linear with fixed coefficients. This may appear to be a very crude approximation. In equation (15) the coefficients depend in particular on the density $f(\bar{y})$ and this may vary very much from one situation to another. Consider for instance the extreme case in which βL is known exactly; then $F(x)$ would be equal to 1 for all $x \geq \beta L$; but for x smaller than βL, $F(x)$ would be equal to the probability that $d \leq x$; when x tends to βL from below, $F(x)$ would usually tend to a number smaller than 1. In this case the density $f(\bar{y})$ would typically be positive for $\bar{y} < \beta L$, would not exist (would be infinite) for $\bar{y} = \beta L$ and would be zero for $\bar{y} \geqq \beta L$; in other words equation (15) would only apply to the extent that capacity $\bar{y}$ is smaller than the productivity βL of the full labour force. Similarly, the coefficient of δw in (15) appears to be very sensitive to the margin between net labour productivity and unit labour cost.

If we stick to a linear equation it is not only for simplicity's sake but also for two other reasons. First, as is usually the case, aggregation over firms smooths out discontinuities that the consideration of a representative firm reveals. Second, we cannot pretend that our study would apply to a wide range of variation of the variables; it is intended to be used only in a domain that does not extend very far from Walrasian equilibrium.

In the dynamic study we shall keep equation (16) unchanged, whatever the regime under consideration, whether it be stationary or subject to significant fluctuations, whether it be predominantly Keynesian or classical. In other words, we shall implicitly assume that the probability function F is subject only to horizontal shifts. This amounts to neglecting an important feedback from the regime observed to the formation of expectations: if the regime tends towards a stationary state, uncertainty about the future demand for goods and the future supply of labour decreases. If this feedback can be neglected in an inquiry that has to cover a vast domain and wants to remain simple, it is because our concern is not long-term growth but rather the relationship between one short-term equilibrium and a few following ones.

In the derivation of equation (16) we made rather strong hypotheses about the formation of expectations concerning the real wage rate and the average level of the variable $\hat{y}$; but we also assumed that present investment would fully raise capacity to its required level. These are of course special hypotheses, explaining why distributed lags do not appear in the equation. Again, simplicity was the main reason for this. It should be noted, however, that this equation permits other combinations of hypotheses on expectations formation and on capacity building.

For instance equation (14) assumes that investment will fully adapt capacity to its desired level. This is, of course, not realistic if we speak of the investment done during a year, even if a lag is introduced between the decision to invest and its implementation. But we shall in the following discussion not take b as being the capital–output ratio; indeed, we shall assume it to be a much lower number, so that the investment decided on during one period will be only a fraction of the difference between desired and existing capital stocks.

Before we proceed, we have still to consider what kind of econometric support can be given to the relationship between profitability and investment. The situation in this respect is indeed rather strange. That such a relationship holds has always been taken for granted by the general public and by most economists. The econometricians, however, often remain rather dubious about it: they have found the dominant factor of investment to be the accelerator, i.e. the need for new capacity when demand for a product expands; the roles played by other factors have been the object of disputes whose outcome is still uncertain. Although definitely correlated with profitability, these potential secondary factors do not include this notion as such; they are in particular past profits, labour cost and capital cost.

One may well argue that the reason for such a state of affairs lies in the fact that profitability is not identified by any measurable quantity. The econometrician naturally gives more credence to well recognized regressions than to supposed relationships between non-measured entities.

It is noteworthy, however, that recent developments in investment econometrics are in the direction of recognizing some role for profitability. It has been argued, perhaps not convincingly, that this was one feature of the so-called 'neo-classical theory of investment'. But above all, the work recently stimulated by James Tobin may be interpreted in this manner.

He claims that a significant explanatory factor of a firm's investment ought to be the ratio q between its stock market evaluation and the replacement cost of its net capital. Whereas his argument stresses portfolio decisions by the managers of the firm, it could equally well be formulated in terms of decisions concerning the real capital stock and its productive capacity. Clearly, the stock market value of a firm is related to its profitability and q was found to have explanatory power for investment both in cross-sections and aggregate time series. Actually, a recent and careful study of quarterly series for US non-financial corporations from 1952 to 1976 leads to a regression that has essentially the same structure as equation (16), with a term in q corresponding to profitability and a term measuring the degree of capacity utilization.[5] It is not inappropriate to take this study as providing an econometric support for equation (16).

Tobin's ratio q itself should probably not be taken as an exact measure of profitability as it is perceived by the managers of the firms since there is a strong element of speculation in stock market evaluation. But this q should be a good proxy, at least in the US where the stock market operates on a wide scale and with better information than in other countries.

Similarly, the term $\beta - e - w$ of equation (16) cannot claim to be more than a proxy for profitability, as the above derivation of this equation has shown. It might even be a rather poor proxy if used in econometric work. But it is an appropriate one for the type of theoretical exploration that is attempted here.

To sum up, equation (16) seems to be the simplest one that permits simultaneous consideration of profitability effects (its first term), with aggregate demand effects (its second term). It neglects a number of aspects that have to be taken into account

[5] G. M. von Furstenberg, 'Corporate investment: does market valuation matter in the aggregate?' *Brookings Papers on Economic Activity*, no. 2, 1977.

in applied studies: distributed lags, substitutability between labour and capital, financial constraints. It may, however, be taken as appropriate for the particular purpose of this book.

The Walrasian stationary equilibrium

In the first chapter the appropriate income distribution for an economy was loosely defined as slowly evolving along a regular path and as sustaining a capital accumulation from which full employment growth could follow. In the simple model studied here such an income distribution clearly is the one associated with a stationary Walrasian equilibrium. It may be very easily defined and discussed. This also provides an opportunity for looking at all characteristics of the Walrasian equilibrium and for making sure that it is free from inconsistencies.

The Walrasian equilibrium was defined by the condition:

$$y = d = \bar{y} = \beta L = \hat{y} \tag{17}$$

A precondition for the existence of a Walrasian stationary equilibrium is that the exogenous labour force L and its productivity β be constant over time, as we shall assume.

Then, the existence of a stationary state requires in particular that the productive capacity $\bar{y}$ be constant and that net investment i be zero. Since we have the investment function (16), this implies:

$$w = \beta - e \tag{18}$$

(as long as (17) is also true). The real cost of labour per unit of output is then equal to $1 - e/\beta$ and the real profit margin equal to e/β. Since γ designates the inverse of the capital–output ratio, the real net rate of return on capital is given by:

$$\rho = \frac{e\gamma}{\beta} \tag{19}$$

Equations (18) and (19) define the appropriate income distribution as a direct consequence of investment behaviour:

the real cost of labour must be such as to induce a zero level of net investment when capacity is equal to output. Such a very simple relationship is not surprising today when we hear so many public declarations stating that investment depends on profitability. But just for this reason it may be worth discussing.

The logic behind the investment function (16) is the uncertainty about the future state of supply and demand in a situation in which there is strict complementarity between capital and labour and no financial constraint. We shall come back to the latter hypotheses in the last chapter and show that they do not grossly mislead us in our representation of the investment function.

The parameter e in the appropriate income distribution may be directly related to the cost of capacity q and to the probability $F(\bar{y})$ that is given to the event that d or βL be smaller than $\bar{y}$. Indeed, in the Walrasian stationary equilibrium, equation (11) may be written as:

$$e = \frac{\beta q}{1 - F(\bar{y})} \qquad (20)$$

Hence, e may be seen to increase with q and with $F(\bar{y})$. But this relation is difficult to interpret as long as no complete model of the determination of the stationary equilibrium has been built. We do not even know which variables should be taken as exogenous at this stage.

Moreover, there may seem to be an element of contradiction between the two hypotheses that a stationary equilibrium is achieved but that firms' decisions are essentially dependent on uncertainties about the future.

Once again, it must be remembered that we do not want to study here long-term growth but only the dynamic links between short-term equilibria so as to draw valid conclusions about medium-term implications of current decisions. The Walrasian stationary equilibrium must not be considered as providing a description of any real economic evolution in itself, but rather as a simple and useful characteristic of a formal model for the study of medium-term dynamics. In these circumstances it is admissible to consider as given the type and degree of uncertainty that firms consider as affecting their future activity.

We shall also take e, or equivalently ρ, as given at this stage and consider (20) as a consistency condition between e, q, βL (equal to $\bar{y}$ in the Walrasian stationary equilibrium) and the function $F(x)$ that would represent firms' expectations in situations in which y and d would be (temporarily) equal to βL.

In other words the 'appropriate income distribution' will be taken as exogenous in the present inquiry, which will be devoted to a study of the role of deviations of the real wage rate from its appropriate level. That we should make such an assumption suggests that finding the appropriate wage rate in a given actual economy is not easy and would require a better knowledge of investment behaviour than is usually available.

But we have not yet considered a full model and we must check that the exogenously given e is compatible with transfer flows and with saving behaviour. We remember in particular the Harrod–Domar difficulty and we know from Nicolas Kaldor that a way of solving it is precisely to find an income distribution that will make required saving equal to warranted saving. This difficulty would indeed render our exogeneity assumption untenable if we did not have the possibility either of choosing, exogenously and in conformity with e, a parameter of income transfers, or of taking advantage of the fact that the saving behaviour assumed here is less crude than that of the Harrod–Domar model.

In the Walrasian stationary equilibrium, with full employment and zero net investment, equilibrium in the goods market requires:

$$r(w, h, m) + g = \beta L \qquad (21)$$

Once w and βL are given, this relation imposes a consistency requirement between the three variables h, m and g. If saving behaviour were not subject to a real wealth effect (i.e. if m did not occur in the consumption function), we should have to consider (21) as a condition on g and h. Here, we shall rather take it as a condition on m, i.e. on the equilibrium value of the households' real wealth.

Taking then h, g as exogenous, private consumption c as equal to $\beta L - g$ and private wealth m as determined by (21), we still have to consider how the economic accounts of table 1 can be fully balanced. In order to do so, we shall accept the possibility that, in the so-called Walrasian stationary equilibrium, the price level increases at a constant rate π, which need not necessarily be zero. We then must add to (21) the following four independent balancing equations (the last balancing equation will then directly follow from the arithmetical necessity known among economists as 'Walras law').

$$\left.\begin{aligned} z &= h+t \\ m &= m_f + m_g \\ wL+z &= \beta L + \pi m_f \\ g &= t + \pi m_g \end{aligned}\right\} \quad (22)$$

Taking h, g, w, β, L and m as given at this stage, these equations can be understood as leaving one degree of freedom in the choice of z, t, m_f, m_g, and π. In the following discussion we shall have to refer again to the 'equilibrium rate of inflation' but not to the specific values of z, t, m_f and m_g, which will then be assumed to be implicitly determined by equations (22).

There is not much more to say about these equations except for three comments. First, we must recall that the real transfers z paid by firms and the real transfers h received by households include the distribution of profits. Making directly an assumption of exogeneity on h is admissible for an inquiry concerning medium-term phenomena but bypasses a precise study of the financing of investment and government consumption; we know, however, from equations (22) that no hidden inconsistency results from such an assumption.

Second, the rate of inflation cannot be taken independently of the exogenous variables L, β, e, g and h. Indeed, equations (18) and (22) imply:

$$h+g = eL+\pi m \tag{23}$$

For a given appropriate income distribution (w and e given), for a given budgetary policy (g and h given), equation (21) determines the equilibrium level of real assets m; equation (23) then gives the rate of inflation π that is required to balance government finance.

Third, the fact that e, g and h occur as exogenous variables points to the fact that different long-term budgetary and financial policies are usually associated with different Walrasian stationary equilibria, each one of them assuming permanently maintained values of these instruments.

To sum up, let us remind ourselves that, in the following discussion, we shall explicitly take as independent exogenous variables L, β, e, g and h. The equilibrium rate of inflation and real wealth of consumers will then be determined, which means that one degree of freedom will still remain for z, t, m_f and m_g, which will not appear explicitly.

3 The sequence of short-term equilibria

A simple model of medium-term economic evolution will now be built and studied. It will present a theoretical justification of the possibility of a stable Keynesian depression. It will also exhibit arguments explaining first why classical unemployment might last for some time, although it cannot be maintained in the long run, second why classical unemployment tends to lead to Keynesian unemployment.

The investment function, which has been defined in the preceding chapter, is of course an essential element of the dynamic model. So also is the consumption function, which implicitly defines households saving. But the model must also contain a representation of the spontaneous changes of prices and wages. These changes will be explained by excess demands and supplies.

This chapter concerns spontaneous evolutions that would appear if the economy were not subject to external perturbations and if no corrective policies were adopted. Such *corrective policies* will be briefly considered in the next chapter. With respect to the dynamic process studied here they will appear as shocks, which suddenly change the value of one variable or another. In particular prices and incomes policies will be interpreted as implying forced exogenous variations in the endogenous variables P and w. Needless to say, the questions as to whether such policies are feasible and as to which conditions are required for their implementation lie outside the scope of this book, even though they are very important in practice.[1]

The short-term equilibrium

The first step towards an analysis of a dynamic process is to characterize the equilibrium that will obtain in each period, depending on the conditions prevailing in that period.

Since we accept the idea of fixed prices in the short run, the prevailing price level P and real wage rate w now appear as exogenous variables. Similarly the productive capacity $\bar{y}$ and the consumers' real assets m are given in the current period, as a consequence of past evolution. In addition to these, four variables, L, β, e, g and h, which have already been taken as exogenous in the study of Walrasian stationary equilibrium, are also given. The short-term equilibrium determines output y, aggregate demand d, the unemployment rate u and other endogenous variables; these quantities are assumed to bear the burden of making decisions mutually consistent in the short run.

Comparative statics

Since the study of short-term equilibrium is not the main concern here, we shall restrict our comparative statics analysis to variations in government consumption g (representative of demand management policy) and in the real wage rate w (representative of prices and incomes policy). To simplify the notation we shall then omit from the equations the exogenous

---

[1] Prices and incomes policies are notoriously difficult to implement. A long history of failures of such policies can be told. But they have been found effective in a number of cases; governments often rely on them and economic advisers themselves must sometimes recommend them. Hence, I cannot accept the view of many theoretical economists according to which prices and incomes policies do not deserve attention.

variables m and h. The basic relations defining the equilibrium,[2] then, are

$$\left.\begin{array}{l} d = r(w) - us(w) + a(\beta - e - w) + b(\hat{y} - \bar{y}) + g \\[2mm] y = \mathrm{Min}(\hat{y}, \bar{y}) \qquad \hat{y} = \mathrm{Min}(d, \beta L) \\[2mm] u = 1 - \dfrac{y}{\beta L} \end{array}\right\} (1)$$

In these four equations, d, y, $\hat{y}$ and u are the endogenous variables.

In order to determine the equilibrium one should proceed in two steps:

(i) find whether it is Keynesian, classical, or inflationary;

(ii) compute the values of endogenous variables for the case that applies and draw the relevant corresponding comparative statics conclusions.

The second step is simpler than the first one. For simplicity in exposition we shall deal with it first; in other words, we shall consider the equations ruling each one of the three types of equilibrium before finding out which type applies. Then the reader who finds the technical discussion of step (i) tiresome will be able to skip it.

If the equilibrium is *Keynesian*, then d is smaller than $\bar{y}$ and βL. The equation for the determination of y is easily derived:

$$y = r(w) - \left[1 - \frac{y}{\beta L}\right] s(w) + a(\beta - e - w) + b(y - \bar{y}) + g \quad (2)$$

Output y increases with government consumption g if

$$\frac{1}{k} = 1 - \frac{s(w)}{\beta L} - b > 0 \tag{3}$$

which we shall assume, as is traditionally done in multiplier

---

[2] In the study of the sequence of equilibria we shall actually assume that investment depends on previous values of $\hat{y}$ and $\bar{y}$. Hence the corresponding short-term equilibrium will be simpler, as if $b = 0$ in system (1). But it will be illuminating to avoid the simplification for the time being.

theory.[3] Since s is positive, this implies in particular $b < 1$. The multiplier is then precisely k.

Output also increases with the real wage rate w if

$$r'_w - us'_w - a > 0 \tag{4}$$

that is if raising w stimulates consumption demand more than it depresses investment demand. Since the latter effect is usually considered as holding, we shall assume (4) also. (This inequality, which involves the endogenous variable u, is assumed to hold for all cases that will be considered.)

If the equilibrium is *classical*, then capacity $\bar{y}$ is smaller than d and βL. Output is equal to capacity; the unemployment rate u is directly given by the last of equations (1). Since capacity is given, the demand for goods is rationed; neither demand management nor incomes policy can do anything to change output and unemployment in the short run. This is of course a consequence of the special assumptions of strict complementarity and fixed labour supply made here.

If the equilibrium is *inflationary*, then βL is smaller than d and $\bar{y}$. There is full employment; output y is restricted to βL by the available labour force and its productivity. Again changes of g or w have no impact on the short-term equilibrium values of y and u.

In order to discuss now what type of equilibrium applies, we must distinguish two cases depending on whether productive capacity $\bar{y}$ is smaller or larger than full employment output βL.

Case in which productive capacity is low ($\bar{y} < \beta L$)

There will certainly be unemployment. It may be Keynesian

---

[3] A well-known exception is found in Kaldor's trade cycle model, where the investment equation was non-linear and the marginal propensity to invest (with respect to income) was supposed to be higher than the marginal propensity to save for intermediate values of y (see N. Kaldor, 'A model of the trade cycle', *Economic Journal*, March 1940). The type of instability that would have resulted from such a hypothesis has apparently not been found in econometric work.

or classical. The type of equilibrium depends on a comparison between d and $\bar{y}$.

To make this comparison, it is convenient to compute three functions of the exogenous variables. The first one $\hat{d}$ is the level that demand would achieve if d were smaller than $\bar{y}$ (hence $y = \hat{y} = \hat{d}$). It is given by:

$$\left(1 - \frac{s}{\beta L} - b\right)\hat{d} = r - s - b\bar{y} + f \tag{5}$$

in which for simplicity we do not exhibit the dependence between r or s and w, and in which we define:

$$f = g + a(\beta - e - w) \tag{6}$$

The second one $\bar{d}$ is the value of d for the case in which $\bar{y} < d < \beta L$, hence $y = \bar{y}$ and $\hat{y} = \bar{d}$:

$$(1 - b)\bar{d} = r - s - b\bar{y} + f + \frac{s}{\beta L}\bar{y} \tag{7}$$

The third one $\tilde{d}$ is the value of d for the case in which $\bar{y} < \beta L < d$, hence $y = \bar{y}$ and $\hat{y} = \beta L$:

$$\tilde{d} = r - s - b\bar{y} + f + \frac{s}{\beta L}\bar{y} + b\beta L \tag{8}$$

The preceding definitions immediately imply:

$$\left(1 - \frac{s}{\beta L} - b\right)(\hat{d} - \bar{y}) = (1 - b)(\bar{d} - \bar{y}) = (\tilde{d} - \bar{y}) - b(\beta L - \bar{y}) \tag{9}$$

Now, suppose $\bar{d} < \bar{y}$, it follows from (9) that we must also have $\hat{d} < \bar{y}$ and $\tilde{d} < \beta L$; therefore in this case we must have $d < \bar{y} < \beta L$ and $y = d = \hat{d}$; the equilibrium is Keynesian. Suppose on the contrary $\bar{d} > \bar{y}$, then $\hat{d} > \bar{y}$ and also $\tilde{d} > \bar{y}$; the equilibrium cannot be Keynesian; it is necessarily classical with $y = \bar{y}$ (whether $d = \bar{d}$ or $d = \tilde{d}$ does not matter for this conclusion).

In other words the equilibrium will be Keynesian or

classical depending on whether or not the exogenous variables are such that:

$$r + f - \left(1 - \frac{\bar{y}}{\beta L}\right)s < \bar{y} \tag{10}$$

This is a condition on the exogenous variables w, h, m, g, $\bar{y}$. Particular attention will be given later to revisions of the real wage rate w and of the price level P, which determine the real wealth by $m = M/P$. Hence it is worth seeing for which values of (P, w) (10) does hold, the other exogenous variables, h, M, g and $\bar{y}$, being kept constant. This is done in figure 1, where the real wage rate is assumed to be below the value $\alpha > \beta$ that would make any production unprofitable, even in the short

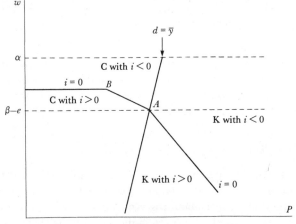

Fig. 1

run (the regions where Keynesian unemployment occurs are denoted by K, those with classical unemployment are denoted by C). Keynesian unemployment holds on the right-hand side. Its region expands toward the left as $\bar{y}$ increases and contracts to the right as g, h or M increases (private consumption is of course an increasing function of h and m). The borderline between the regions of Keynesian and classical unemployment obtains when inequality (10) is replaced by an equality. It is an upward sloping line since small variations δP and δw along this line must obey:

$$\frac{1}{k}\delta y = (r'_w - us'_w - a)\,\delta w - (r'_m - us'_m)m\frac{\delta P}{P} = 0 \quad (11)$$

and we have assumed both brackets to be positive.

For the study of dynamic shifts from one short-term equilibrium to the next one it is interesting to identify the conditions under which capacity $\bar{y}$ will expand, i.e. the conditions under which net investment i is positive.[4]

At the point A, at which $y = \bar{y} = \hat{y}$ and $w = \beta - e$, net investment is zero. In the neighbourhood of this point and in the region of Keynesian unemployment $i = \delta i > 0$ if and only if:

$$-a\,\delta w + b\,\delta y > 0$$

which obtains for some negative values of δw (since $\delta\hat{d} > 0$).

More generally, the region in which net investment is positive is as shown in figure 1. It is below the line $i = 0$ passing through points B and A. A detailed construction of this line would be out of place here.[5]

Case in which productive capacity is high ($\beta L < \bar{y}$)

When productive capacity exceeds full employment output, classical unemployment cannot hold (at least as long as we assume that the real labour cost is not high enough to make any production unprofitable, even in the short run, when capacity

---

[4] If investment did not depend on the current values of $\hat{y}$ and $\bar{y}$ but on their previous values, as we shall assume later, the line $i = 0$ would be replaced by a horizontal line.

[5] Figure 1 is drawn under the assumption:

$$a > kb(r'_w - us'_w - a)$$

which will be assumed to hold (if not, the intersection of the region of Keynesian unemployment with the region of positive net investment would be quite small). Passing through point B from right to left one shifts from $\bar{y} < d < \beta L$ to $\bar{y} < \beta L < d$, hence from $\hat{y} = d$ to $\hat{y} = \beta L$.

is available). Hence, either Keynesian unemployment or inflation prevails, depending on whether or not aggregate demand d is short of full employment output βL.

To compare d with βL it is convenient to compute not only $\hat{d}$, defined by the exogenous variables in (5), but also d^+ (which gives demand under conditions of inflation), defined by:

$$d^+ = r + b(\beta L - \bar{y}) + f \qquad (12)$$

This definition implies

$$\left(1 - \frac{s}{\beta L} - b\right)(\hat{d} - \beta L) = d^+ - \beta L \qquad (13)$$

Hence, $d^+ < \beta L$ implies $\hat{d} < \beta L$: inflation cannot hold and Keynesian unemployment must hold. Conversely, $d^+ > \beta L$ implies $\hat{d} > \beta L$ and the short-term equilibrium is inflationary. In other words, the necessary and sufficient condition for Keynesian unemployment is:

$$r + f + b(\beta L - \bar{y}) < \beta L \qquad (14)$$

This condition on the exogenous variables is represented in figure 2 for varying P and w, but for fixed h, M, g and $\bar{y}$. The

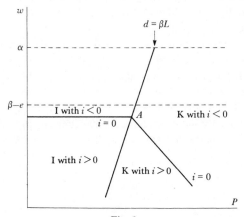

Fig. 2

border line between the regions of Keynesian unemployment and of inflation is an upward sloping line along which:

$$\frac{1}{k}\delta y = (r'_w - a)\,\delta w - r'_m \frac{\delta P}{P} = 0 \tag{15}$$

Figure 2 also exhibits the region in which net investment is positive. When inflation holds $\hat{y} = \beta L$ and the condition is immediately derived from the investment function:

$$w < \beta - e - \frac{b}{a}(\bar{y} - \beta L) \tag{16}$$

When Keynesian unemployment prevails the condition on w is more severe since $\hat{y} = d$ and excess capacity $\bar{y} - \hat{y}$ is still larger. This explains the kink in the line $i = 0$ at A.

The dynamic links

In the short-term equilibrium, assets and prices are given, whereas in a longer-term perspective they are the result of past accumulation or past forces which pushed prices in one direction or another. In our simple model this means that the four variables $\bar{y}$, m, P and w, which were taken as exogenous for the short-term equilibrium, have to be explained when a sequence of equilibria is considered.

For the representation of this sequence, we take time as being a succession of periods: $\ldots t-1, t, t+1 \ldots$ We must also now be more precise about the timing of variables than we have been previously.

Capital accumulation poses no new problem because it is the direct result of current behaviour, which has already been formalized. On the contrary we shall have to be specific about changes in the price level and in the real wage rate.

Capital accumulation

The accumulation of capital has two sides: (i) investment

resulting in a change in productive capacity, (ii) changes in private wealth that affect the demand for goods by consumers. These two sides respectively concern $\bar{y}$ and m.

Changes in productive capacity result from net investment according to

$$\bar{y}_{t-1} = \bar{y}_t + \gamma i_t \tag{17}$$

in which γ is the reciprocal of the capital–output ratio. In order to take some account of the often long lags between investment decisions and their completion, we shall assume from now on that investment depends on the previous values of the variables affecting it. Hence, we shall write:

$$i_t = a(\beta - e - w_{t-1}) + b(\hat{y}_{t-1} - \bar{y}_{t-1}) \tag{18}$$

This means that productive capacity for period t will not depend on the values of the real wage rate and aggregate demand after period $t-2$.

The timings assumed in equations (17) and (18) are, of course, very crude in comparison with what econometric studies of investment and of productive capacities imply. The introduction of distributed lags would make the formalization more realistic, but more cumbersome also. This does not seem to be worth the trouble for the kind of theoretical exploration that is attempted here.

If we want to visualize (17) and (18) as simple representations of concrete phenomena, we must, however, admit that the unit period is rather long, something like a year rather than a quarter. We shall keep that in mind.

Changes in the real wealth m_t of consumers will result from changes of their nominal wealth and of the price level:

$$m_{t+1} - m_t = \frac{1}{P_{t+1}}[(M_{t+1} - M_t) - (P_{t+1} - P_t)m_t] \tag{19}$$

Since $M_{t+1} - M_t$ is the nominal saving by consumers during period t, it is also equal to $W_t - H_t - C_t$ or to $P_t[(w_t y_t)/\beta +$

$(h - c_t)$], if the assumption is made that the exogenous real net transfer h is constant. Hence:

$$m_{t+1} - m_t = \left[\frac{w_t y_t}{\beta} + h - c_t - \frac{P_{t+1} - P_t}{P_t} m_t \right] \frac{P_t}{P_{t+1}} \qquad (20)$$

in which real consumption depends on the type of equilibrium. If the demand for goods by consumers is not rationed, i.e. if a Keynesian equilibrium holds, then

$$c_t = r(w_t, h, m_t) - u_t s(w_t, h, m_t) \qquad (21)$$

As mentioned earlier, the fact that h is exogenous (and constant) is a simplification. The real value of the taxes paid by consumers is positively correlated with employment and real wage rates. Transfers from government to households is negatively correlated with employment. The distribution of profits to households is positively correlated with employment but negatively with the pressure on capacity, because of the need for investment financing; its correlation with the real wage rate is obscure because an increase of this rate reduces profits (for a given level of demand) but also reduces investment. Since these correlations are complex and often act in opposite directions, the assumption of exogeneity is probably less serious than it might seem at first.

The price level

How should we now specify changes in the price level P and in the real wage rate w from one temporary equilibrium to another?

One sometimes sees it suggested that the specification should be derived from a theoretical model explaining the behaviour of the agents: price and wage changes are decided by firms as a rational reaction to the situation confronting them. These decisions should be formalized and the formalization would give the required equations of the dynamic model.

It is difficult to believe one could rely only, or even mainly, on such an approach. Mathematical economics is certainly powerful. But the research of the past ten years into what has been called 'the microeconomic foundations of macro-economics' has shown how difficult it is to model complex situations in which many decisions are taken. If we try to build a theoretical microeconomic model in order to find out the dynamics of changes in such macrophenomena as the price level or the purchasing power of the hourly wage, we may be fairly certain that we shall end up with a very partial representation of the real world; the representation will be so partial that the adequacy of the derived dynamic specification will be quite doubtful.

We must of course start from the best possible knowledge of the relevant phenomena. At present this derives from the many econometric equations that have been fitted to actual data on macroeconomic price and wage changes. Such equations may be criticized on the grounds that their theoretical foundations are weak, loose or obscure. But, to the extent that they give a good fit, they are to be preferred to supposedly rigorous specifications derived from very abstract theoretical models. For revisions in prices and wages, the proper combination of observation and logical deduction often at present favours reliance on an econometric equation rather than on a purely theoretical equation.

In our present attempt we should not, however, feel obliged to write the equations as they are found in econometric articles. We must simplify them so as to build an easily manageable model. In particular we must forget about the distributed lags that play an important role in econometric specifications. At least at this stage, taking such lags into account would complicate matters too much.

We have learnt from econometric studies that prices and wages are fairly interdependent, that they react to excess demand or supply both in the goods markets and in the labour markets and that moreover such reactions have a fair degree of asymmetry.

We must therefore introduce into our equation for the spontaneous change of the price level both the excess demand for goods E_1 and the excess demand for labour E_2, these two quantities being either positive or negative. We shall stick to a simple formula by making the relation linear for each type of equilibrium and therefore write:

$$\frac{P_{t+1}-P_t}{P_t} = \pi + \lambda_1 E_{1t} + \lambda_2 E_{2t} \qquad (22)$$

Three comments about this equation are in order. First, the constant term π appears as a kind of expected inflation rate that would occur if supply equalled demand in both markets (i.e. in the case of a short-term Walrasian equilibrium). It is taken as constant in this formulation although expectations about inflation depend on past rates of inflation. But neglect of distributed lags makes it impossible to take this fact into account; moreover in a study which considers medium-term impacts rather than longer-term consequences, such a simplification may still be an admissible hypothesis. Since the representation of expectations about inflation would be weak here in any case, we shall in the following discussion take π to be zero.

In the second place, it is commonly held that the impact of excess demand or supply on the price level exhibits a strong asymmetry: excess demand pushes up prices much more than an equal excess supply would lower them. The linear equation (22) would not permit such an asymmetry if it is applied independently of the type of equilibrium appearing in period t. But we shall take different values of the coefficient λ_1 (or λ_2) depending on whether the excess demand E_{1t} (or E_{2t}) is positive or negative: λ_1 will be much larger in the first case than in the second.

Finally, the definition of what is meant by excess demand or excess supply is not always obvious in the theory of fixed price equilibria. This is well recognized.[6] Here we must be precise if

---

[6] See in particular *The Theory of Unemployment Reconsidered*.

we want to have a full specification. This is why equation (22) will be rewritten for each of the three types of equilibrium.

If classical unemployment holds in period t, there is an excess demand for goods and this is naturally written as $d_t - y_t$; but there is also an excess supply of labour $L - y_t/\beta$. We shall write:

$$\frac{P_{t+1} - P_t}{P_t} = \mu(d_t - y_t) - v(\beta L - y_t) \tag{23}$$

In the case of inflation, in which firms are constrained on the labour market but would like to produce up to capacity $\bar{y}_t$ or at least up to demand d_t, the excess demand for goods is again $d_t - y_t$, whereas the demand for labour is, except for the multiplier $1/\beta$, equal to the minimum of $\bar{y}_t$ and d_t. Hence, the change in the price level is equal to:

$$\frac{P_{t+1} - P_t}{P_t} = \mu(d_t - y_t) + \rho[\text{Min}(d_t, \bar{y}_t) - \beta L] \tag{24}$$

It is understood that ρ is much larger than v.

When Keynesian unemployment holds, the excess supply of labour is $L - y_t/\beta$. The supply of goods by firms depends on their capacity and labour constraints; it may be said to be the minimum of $\bar{y}_t$ and βL. Hence:

$$\frac{P_{t+1} - P_t}{P_t} = -\lambda[\text{Min}(\bar{y}_t, \beta L) - y_t] - v(\beta L - y_t) \tag{25}$$

The positive number λ must be much smaller than μ.

The real wage rate

After these equations concerning changes in the price level, we must consider the changes in the real wage rate.

The formalization we are looking for must follow from what we know about the 'Phillips curve' and from what has been assumed above about changes in price level. Considering the results of econometric studies we must, however, first remember that our time unit is more like a year than a quarter and second that the present model sharply distinguishes types of equilibria whereas real situations always have a mixed character.

This said, it is pretty clear that the real wage rate ought to decrease in a situation of classical unemployment. Excess demand in the goods market and excess supply in the labour market create a situation in which the increase of nominal wages must lag behind the increase in prices.

What has to be assumed in situations of Keynesian unemployment and of inflation is less obvious. Here we shall agree with Keynes in saying that, when excess supply prevails on all markets, there is no clear tendency in the real wage. In a situation of inflation, on the other hand, we shall say that the real wage rate drifts upwards. The combination of these two hypotheses is compatible with econometric studies showing that, in modern industrial countries, the impact of demand pressure is much stronger in the labour market than in the goods market. The asymmetry of this impact acts to favour an upward bias in real wage changes. Observation moreover shows that periods of demand inflation are periods during which real wages increase particularly fast.

In order to give a mathematical expression to the preceding hypotheses, which will of course play an important role in the subsequent analysis, and to have, however, simple formulas, we shall assume that, except for exogenous shifts:

– in the case of classical unemployment:

$$w_{t+1} = w_t - \sigma u_t \qquad (26)$$

σ being a positive coefficient;

– in the case of inflation:

$$w_{t+1} = w_t + \tau[\mathrm{Min}(d_t, \bar{y}_t) - \beta L] \qquad (27)$$

τ being a positive constant;

– in the case of Keynesian unemployment:

$$w_{t+1} = w_t \qquad (28)$$

The simplicity of these hypotheses is recognized and is responsible for some features of the model.[7] For instance, if we refer back to figures 1 and 2 and consider the change $w_{t+1} - w_t$ induced, for a given level w_t, by various values of P_t, we can see that, moving on a horizontal line from right to left:

– in the case of figure 1, the change is zero in the Keynesian region, but steps down to a constant negative value in the classical region;

– in the case of figure 2, the change is again zero in the Keynesian region, then goes up progressively in the inflationary region as long as $d_t < \bar{y}_t$ and finally remains at a constant positive value when $d_t \geqq \bar{y}_t$.

It would have been possible to assume smoother variations for the adjustment of real wages, but at the cost of added complexity and without any substantial gain in the understanding of the phenomena. We shall, however, not forget in the next section the nature of the simplifications assumed here.

Moreover, it must be recognized that the dynamic process defined in this section does not take account of changes in expectations that may occur as a result of prolonged trends in one direction or another. This process operates on a small number of macrovariables and relates their values in one

[7] The process assumed here is, of course, too simple to do justice to the complex econometrics of real wage changes. In a number of cases unemployment has been found to have depressed real wages whereas generalized excess supply prevailed in the goods market. On the other hand this depressing effect seems to be mainly a temporary one, connected with the lags in the determination of nominal wages; it has its own limit and cannot prevail for a long time. Verbal reference will be made later to a process in which something like equation (26), with a smaller numerical value of σ, would prevail in a regime of Keynesian unemployment. Hence, the author will perhaps be excused for the oversimplification that equation (28) contains.

period to their values in the preceding period. It has no memory beyond this immediate link. The formulation is definitely weak with respect to the rational reaction of agents to a durable change in their environment. This remark concerns saving and investment behaviour as well as revisions in the price level or in the real wage rate.

This is why the dynamic process cannot be appropriate for the representation of long-term phenomena and can only be a useful approximation for medium-term studies, those concerning spontaneous evolution during a small number of successive years.

The Keynesian depression

We must now begin the study of the medium-term dynamics of our model. Whenever necessary for simplicity, we shall assume that we are in the neighbourhood of a Walrasian stationary equilibrium. Indeed, we have stated in chapter 1 that the fixed price temporary general equilibrium with rationing approach would lose its force if the excess demands or supplies are large.

We begin with the discussion of a depression in which unemployment is due to the lack of a sufficient demand for goods. We shall concentrate our attention on the case in which, if a corrective economic policy is not adopted and if, more generally, exogenous variables remain constant, the depression tends to persist indefinitely. Roughly speaking we may say that the economy moves toward a stable stationary Keynesian equilibrium; at least this is true for real quantities because the price level may keep changing and will in particular go down indefinitely if the long-term expected rate of inflation π is zero, the case on which we concentrate our attention for simplicity.[8]

---

[8] The existence and properties of a stable Keynesian stationary state with a permanently decreasing price level were recently studied by S. Honkapohja with a model in which investment was ignored. His results present some similarities with those obtained here. See 'On the dynamics of disequilibria

A Keynesian stationary state

Given equation (28) we now consider a situation in which the real wage rate is constant. We shall moreover focus our attention on the case in which this wage rate w is smaller than $\beta - e$. If it was larger, investment would be negative and capacity would decrease indefinitely so that unemployment would eventually become classical. Before doing anything else we must characterize a *stationary Keynesian equilibrium*.

We shall simplify the equation without losing any real substance by assuming that, in the consumption function, $s(w, h, m)$ is a constant function. Since a stationary state implies that net investment is zero, we can immediately write two equations on the real quantities:

$$\bar{y} = y + \frac{a}{b}(\beta - e - w) \tag{29}$$

$$y = k[r(w, h, m) - s + g] \tag{30}$$

in which k is the constant multiplier given by

$$\frac{1}{k} = 1 - \frac{s}{\beta L} \tag{31}$$

The two equations (29) and (30) involve three endogenous variables: output y, productive capacity $\bar{y}$ and consumers' real wealth m. Consideration of the dynamic adjustment of the price level P and the nominal wealth M will give a third equation in these three variables.

Notice however that, if real wealth effects did not exist, i.e. if the function r did not vary with m, (29) and (30) would fully determine the stationary levels of output and capacity. In the following discussion we shall have to refer to this case; it is

in a macro model with flexible wages and prices', in M. Aoki and A. Mazzolo ed., *New Trends in Dynamic System Theory and Economics*, Proceedings of the Udine conference, Academic Press, 1979; 'The employment multiplier after disequilibrium dynamics in a simple macro model', Harvard Institute of Economic Research, February 1979.

unrealistic, but it will provide an easy reference point for initiating precise studies, which will often be difficult.

Three remarks can be made right away on the implications of the model for the case in which the function r does not depend on m_t and in which, therefore, real wealth effects can be neglected.

Firstly, given the Keynesian stationary equilibrium defined as a solution of (29) and (30), the output level y is determined exactly by the equation that would apply in the short run if investment could be neglected. In other words, adaptation of output to its medium-term equilibrium value is instantaneous except for the accelerator phenomenon.

Secondly, strictly speaking we should no longer consider the solution of (29) and (30) as defining a stationary state, because real wealth will normally decrease without converging to any positive limit value. Hence, the process cannot be sustained indefinitely and real wealth effects will sooner or later be felt.

Thirdly, the depression of the price level will be purely neutral with respect to aggregate demand, a feature which may be considered as unsatisfactory. This reminds us that, in the model, the budgetary policy is supposed to act directly on real values, g or h. Hence, the depression of prices does not help to increase the purchasing power of transfers or of the government budget. This is somewhat unrealistic.

In any case, equation (29) alone shows that a Keynesian stationary equilibrium cannot hold unless the real wage rate is smaller than $\beta - e$ and that productive capacity then permanently remains in excess of output; the profitability of new investment is compensated for by this excess capacity.

Equations (20) and (25) determine the change $m_{t+1} - m_t$ in real balances. In the Keynesian stationary equilibrium this change must be zero, which implies:

$$\frac{wy}{\beta} + h - y + g + m[\lambda \operatorname{Min}(\bar{y}, \beta L) + v \beta L - (\lambda + v) y] = 0 \qquad (32)$$

This is the third equation on the endogenous variables, $y, \bar{y}$ and m.

It is worth noting that a state of stationary Keynesian unemployment obtains here, even though the price level is not fully rigid downward. The decrease of prices indeed acts as a favourable influence on real wealth, and hence indirectly on consumption demand; but its action is exactly compensated for by the dissaving that the low output level generates. Some price flexibility does not suffice to get rid of the Keynesian depression.

It might be argued that the assumption of a fully rigid real wage w_t is responsible for this result. Indeed, without it the existence of a stationary Keynesian equilibrium could not be proved in general. But removing this convenient assumption is more likely to lead to a decreasing real wage rate, hence to a situation in which Keynesian unemployment will exhibit a tendency to increase continually, rather than to provide an additional reason for the spontaneous disappearance of unemployment.

In order to clarify this point let us consider again the dynamics of the real wage rate in a state of Keynesian unemployment. On the one hand, w_t tends to decrease because of the excess supply on the labour market; on the other hand, it tends to increase because of the depressing impact excess supply on the goods market imposes on the price level. But there are reasons for thinking that the first effect ought to be stronger than the second one: the sensitivity of the prices of goods to their excess supply seems to have been found weaker than the sensitivity of nominal wages to unemployment; moreover under sustained Keynesian unemployment the degree of excess supply must be larger in the labour market than in the goods market where supply has been depressed by the progressive reduction of productive capacity.

Let us then come back to the assumption of a fixed real wage rate, while bearing in mind that the resulting Keynesian stationary equilibrium is an abstraction that would disappear under a more accurate representation of actual phenomena but which does not make things look more difficult than they are.

'Medium-term' multipliers

One may check that, when $w = \beta - e$, the three equations (29), (30) and (32) have a solution corresponding to a Walrasian stationary equilibrium, with $y = \bar{y} = \beta L$ (account being taken of $g + h = eL$ as given by (23) in chapter 2); the real balance m is then given by the solution of equation (30).

For small variations δw of the real wage rate in the neighbourhood of this Walrasian stationary equilibrium, we may derive the following equations for the Keynesian stationary equilibrium:

$$\delta\bar{y} = \delta y - \frac{a}{b}\delta w$$

$$\delta y = kr'_w\,\delta w + kr'_m\,\delta m \tag{33}$$

$$-\frac{e}{\beta}\delta y + L\delta w + \lambda m\varepsilon\delta\bar{y} - (\lambda + v)m\delta y = 0$$

Where $\varepsilon = 0$ if $\delta\bar{y} \geqq 0$ and $\varepsilon = 1$ if $\delta\bar{y} < 0$.

When real wealth effects are taken into account[9] ($r'_m > 0$), one sees that the first and third of these equations jointly determine δy and $\delta\bar{y}$, whereas the second one determines δm. Moreover, one can see that a solution with $\delta\bar{y} \geqq 0$ and $\delta w < 0$ exists if and only if:

$$\beta L\,\delta w = [e + (\lambda + v)\beta m]\,\delta y \geqq \frac{a}{b}[e + (\lambda + v)\beta m]\,\delta w \tag{34}$$

This requires:

$$\beta L < \frac{a}{b}[e + (\lambda + v)\beta m] \tag{35}$$

---

[9] If $r'_m = 0$, the second equation determines δy and the third equation must be dropped since m_t is not converging, as was mentioned above.

If the reverse inequality holds, the system (33) has the solution:

$$\beta \left[L - \frac{a}{b} \lambda m \right] \delta w = [e + v \, \beta m] \, \delta y \qquad (36)$$

with

$$[e + v \, \beta m] \, \delta \bar{y} = \left\{ \beta L - \frac{a}{b} [e + (\lambda + v) \, \beta m] \right\} \delta w$$

which indeed gives a negative value for $\delta \bar{y}$.

Since, as we shall see, the Keynesian stationary equilibrium can be taken as stable, equation (34), if inequality (35) holds at the Walrasian stationary equilibrium, and equation (36) if it does not, also determine the final outcome of changes in the real wage rate. We may say that *they determine the 'medium-term' consequences* of an incomes policy, acting on the real wage alone,[10] when the change in w is small, when moreover the situation is one of Keynesian stationary equilibrium and is not too far from Walrasian stationary equilibrium.

To speak of the medium term in the present context may be confusing and needs clarification. Indeed, we consider the changes induced in the limiting Keynesian stationary state; to speak of 'long-term consequences' would seem more appropriate at first sight. If we avoid that description here it is in order to stress that the model under consideration does not claim correctly to represent long-term trends; the assumption of a fixed real wage and the lack of a serious treatment of the adjustment of expectations make the model inappropriate for studies of the long term. On the other hand we must recognize that the tendency towards the Keynesian stationary state is likely to be slow since it involves an adjustment of real wealth.

[10] Of course such an incomes policy is an abstraction that can hardly ever be observed. Measures that raise the real wage rate also tend to raise the price level, unless compensation is provided. These measures will therefore usually have in practice a depressing effect on real wealth, which should not be overlooked.

Hence, the so called 'medium-term multipliers' should be understood as abstractions. Considering them helps one to realize why and how the short-term multipliers would be misleading if they were used beyond the current period; but these medium-term multipliers do not really measure anything that could be observed.

It is, then, worth comparing the medium-term impact with the short-term impact of the same change:

$$\delta y = k r'_w \, \delta w \qquad (37)$$

Whereas both impacts have the same sign, they obey quite different rules. One cannot estimate the final effect from the immediate one. If λ and v, which are small, can be neglected, then one can write the medium-term impact:

$$\frac{\delta y}{\beta L} \sim \frac{\delta w}{e} \qquad (38)$$

The medium-term elasticity of output with respect to the real wage would then approach w/e and be typically much larger than one, whereas the short-term elasticity may be taken as smaller than one. (This assumes, of course, the existence of real wealth effects: $r'_m > 0$.)

In the same way we can study the 'medium-term impact' of demand management policy by assuming an exogenous change in either[11] the government demand for goods g or the transfer income to households h.

Considering again the neighbourhood of the Walrasian stationary equilibrium, i.e. a situation in which the value taken by the terms in square brackets in equation (32) is negligible,

---

[11] It is worth noting that the exogenous variables g, h and w appearing in equations (29) to (32) can be chosen independently from one another without this raising any difficulty with the equilibrium of income flows. Indeed, equation (23) of chapter 2, which constrained the choice of exogenous variables for a Walrasian stationary equilibrium, does not apply here. This equation is nothing else than the form taken by (32) at the Walrasian stationary equilibrium when, moreover, $\pi = 0$.

and assuming a small change δg on g with w and h kept fixed, we find:

$$\delta\bar{y} = \delta y = k[\delta g + r'_m \, \delta m] \tag{39}$$

$$\left(\frac{w}{\beta} - 1 - vm\right)\delta y + \delta g = 0 \tag{40}$$

(The last equality corresponds to the case in which the reverse of inequality (35) holds and $\bar{y} \leqq \beta L$; if not, v in (40) ought to be replaced by $\lambda + v$.) The medium-term multiplier is then given by:

$$\delta y = \frac{\beta}{\beta - w + \beta vm} \delta g \tag{41}$$

This is again a quite different formula from the one applying to the short-term multiplier. The difference between the two is explained by the fact that, in the medium term, the real wealth m adjusts, according to (39), to what is required by (40).

Stability analysis

Let us now consider the stability of the Keynesian stationary equilibrium.[12] Holding the values of the exogenous variables constant, we must study the dynamic system that describes the change from the endogenous values $y_{t-1}, \bar{y}_{t-1}, i_{t-1}$ and m_t to $y_t, \bar{y}_t,$ i_t and m_{t+1}. It will be sufficient to take a linear approximation of this system and, considering again the neighbourhood of the Walrasian stationary equilibrium, to neglect terms that would have a second order of smallness with respect to the deviations from this equilibrium.

---

[12] The stability analysis to be discussed now is of course different from the familiar one, which is intended to apply to the quantity adjustment process that operates during the current period leading to the short-term equilibrium. The object of the present analysis is on the contrary the price–quantity process that transforms one short-term equilibrium into the subsequent one.

In this framework we can write directly:

$$\bar{y}_t = \bar{y}_{t-1} + \gamma i_{t-1} \tag{42}$$

$$i_t = by_{t-1} - b\bar{y}_{t-1} + A \tag{43}$$

$$y_t = kby_{t-1} - kb\bar{y}_{t-1} + kr'_m m_t + B \tag{44}$$

in which A and B are constant terms, depending on the values taken by the exogenous variables (it is not necessary to write the expressions of these terms). Similarly, from equations (20), (25) and (44) we derive an approximation for $m_{t+1} - m_t$; hence:

$$m_{t+1} = \tau by_{t-1} + (\lambda m - \tau b)\bar{y}_{t-1} + \gamma \lambda m i_{t-1} + \\ + (1 - \theta kr'_m)m_t + D \tag{45}$$

in which D is again a constant term, whereas the new coefficients τ and θ are given by:

$$\tau = (1 - \theta k)b \quad \theta = 1 - \frac{w}{\beta} + (\lambda + v)m \tag{46}$$

(Equation (45) is written for the case in which $\bar{y}_{t-1} < \beta L$, i.e. the case in which the reverse of inequality (35) holds; if (35) were to apply, then in (45) λm ought to be replaced by zero and the following conclusions would still hold.)

The dynamic system defined by (42) to (45) is conveniently written in matrix form:

$$
\begin{bmatrix} \bar{y}_t \\ y_t \\ i_t \\ m_{t+1} \end{bmatrix}
=
\begin{bmatrix}
1 & 0 & \gamma & 0 \\
-kb & kb & 0 & kr'_m \\
-b & b & 0 & 0 \\
\lambda m - \tau & \tau & \gamma \lambda m & 1 - \theta kr'_m
\end{bmatrix}
\begin{bmatrix} \bar{y}_{t-1} \\ y_{t-1} \\ i_{t-1} \\ m_t \end{bmatrix}
+
\begin{bmatrix} 0 \\ B \\ A \\ D \end{bmatrix}
\tag{47}
$$

Stability of the stationary Keynesian equilibrium is then equivalent to the property that the characteristic roots of the square matrix of this system all have modulus smaller than 1. It so happens that the roots are rather easy to study.

Zero is a root since, multiplying the matrix to the right by the column vector with elements $(1, 1, -1/\gamma, 0)'$, one obtains the null vector. If there were no real wealth effects ($r'_m = 0$), another root would be equal to 1 (multiply to the right by the column vector with elements 0, 0, 0, 1). (We find here that, when $r'_m = 0$, the process is convergent in $y_t, \bar{y}_t$, and i_t but not convergent in m_t; this property has already been mentioned.)

Since the real wealth effects may be taken as positive but small, we can limit attention to an approximation of the roots for small values of $\varepsilon = kr'_m$. More precisely we need a linear approximation in ε for any root that is equal to one when $\varepsilon = 0$, and we may be satisfied with the approximation corresponding to $\varepsilon = 0$ for the roots whose modulus differs from one.

Calculus shows that the root that is close to one is approximately equal to:

$$1 - (\theta - \lambda m)\varepsilon = 1 - \varepsilon\left(1 - \frac{w}{\beta} + vm\right)$$

Since at the Walrasian stationary equilibrium $\varepsilon > 0$, $w < \beta$ and $vm > 0$, this root is smaller than 1.

Considering now the case where $\varepsilon = 0$ in order to find the other roots ξ, we see they obey the following second degree equation:

$$\xi^2 - (1 + kb)\xi + (\gamma + k)b = 0$$

The condition:

$$(\gamma + k)b < 1 \tag{48}$$

is necessary and sufficient (when $\gamma b > 0$) for the two roots to have modulus smaller than 1. This condition may be assumed to hold on the basis of available econometric evidence.

Indeed, not only are the values found for γ, k and b such as to make (48) valid; but also, when $r'_m = 0$, the system defined by (42) to (44) is nothing else than a particular form of the familiar multiplier–accelerator model; and we know that econometric applications of this model have practically always found it stable.

To sum up, let us say (i) that a Keynesian stationary state will appear in our model as a limit for any spontaneous evolution during which Keynesian unemployment permanently prevails, (ii) that in the neighbourhood of such a stationary state the latter condition will hold, but (iii) that convergence is likely to be slow since one of the roots of the dynamic process is not much smaller than 1.

Transient classical unemployment

The spontaneous dynamics of inflation and of classical unemployment are different from that of Keynesian unemployment. Indeed, there cannot be any stationary equilibrium of the classical or inflationary type, even if we refer only to real values, as was accepted when we spoke of stationary Keynesian equilibrium. Unless there is an exogenous shock, the real wage rate falls after any short-term equilibrium with classical unemployment; and it increases after any such equilibrium with inflation.

Moreover, since Keynesian unemployment tends to be stable, we already know that the spontaneous evolution does not tend to restore the Walrasian stationary equilibrium from any initial situation. Hence, it is not very interesting to study whether the latter equilibrium would be stable if approached from a situation of classical or inflationary type.

Concentrating now on classical unemployment we shall argue that it is likely to spontaneously lead to Keynesian unemployment, but that the shift from one type of unemployment to the other is not as fast as one might have thought.

The argument cannot, however, be given rigorously in full generality. We shall have to accept a number of simplifications when proceeding.

Let us first write the dynamic system that applies to classical unemployment. In order to do so, we shall consider the simultaneous variations of the real wage rate w_t, net investment i_t, productive capacity $\bar{y}_t$, demand for goods d_t and real wealth m_t. But, since we may limit attention to the neighbourhood of the Walrasian stationary equilibrium, it will be convenient to consider the differences

$$
\begin{aligned}
z_t &= d_t - \bar{y}_t & \beta L u_t &= \beta L - \bar{y}_t \\
v_t &= w_t - \beta + e & n_t &= m_t - m
\end{aligned}
\tag{49}
$$

in which m refers to the value of real wealth in the Walrasian equilibrium.

Let us write:

$$
d_t = r(w_t, h, m_t) - su_t + i_t + g
$$

or, taking the equilibrium relation of the Walrasian equilibrium into account:

$$
d_t - \beta L = r'_w v_t + r'_m n_t - su_t + i_t
$$

and finally:

$$
z_t = r'_w v_t + r'_m n_t + (\beta L - s)u_t + i_t
\tag{50}
$$

The dynamic system can now be written:

$$
\left.
\begin{aligned}
i_t &= -av_{t-1} + b \operatorname{Min}(z_{t-1}, \beta L u_{t-1}) \\
u_t &= u_{t-1} - \frac{\gamma}{\beta L} i_{t-1} \\
v_t &= v_{t-1} - \sigma u_{t-1} \\
n_{t+1} &= n_t + i_t + L v_t + e L u_t - \mu m z_t + v m \beta L u_t
\end{aligned}
\right\}
\tag{51}
$$

In order to study its dynamic behaviour we shall concentrate attention on the case in which, at date 0, starting from the stationary Walrasian equilibrium, the real wage rate experiences a sudden exogenous increase to $w_1 > \beta - e$ (or $v_1 > 0$). What is the economic evolution starting from such initial conditions?

In the first period $v_1 > 0$ leads to an excess demand for goods $(z_1 = r'_w v_1)$, but $u_1 = i_1 = n_1 = 0$, considering the lags in system (51). Net investment becomes negative in the second period $(i_2 = -av_1)$ and classical unemployment appears in the third period $(u_3 = a\gamma v_1/\beta L)$. From then on, the real wage decreases and the unemployment rate increases, as long as net investment remains negative.

In order to characterize the dynamics of classical unemployment, we can consider the system (51) at period t, taking into account the fact that $z_\tau > 0$ for all $\tau = 1, 2, \ldots, t-1$ and $u_\tau > 0$ for all $\tau = 3, 4, \ldots, t-1$. We would like to show that:

– as long as net investment i_t remains negative, classical unemployment prevails: $z_t > 0$ and $u_t > 0$;

– when i_t has become positive, the unemployment rate is most likely to be positive as long as the excess demand for goods remains positive; in other words, $z_t < 0$ will occur before $u_t < 0$, thus leading to Keynesian unemployment rather than to inflation.

But real wealth effects make the discussion quite involved. In the excess demand for goods, equation (50), they have the sign of n_t and system (51) shows that this sign is strongly dependent on μ, the parameter characterizing the speed of adjustment of the price of goods in reaction to excess demand. For instance, at the beginning, when $v_t > 0$ (and Lv_t may be assumed larger than $-i_t$), the sequence of the n_t will be positive if μ is small, but negative if μ is large enough;[13] intuition and our present knowledge about the likely values of the various parameters do not tell us which one of these two cases should be accepted. Fortunately, we may take it as a fact that r'_m is rather small, so that real wealth effects should not dominate in the determination of the excess demand for goods. We shall therefore proceed with our formal discussion assuming away these effects ($r'_m = 0$). In the case of a speedy adjustment of the

[13] Indeed, real wealth is positively affected by the forced saving that the rationing on the goods market implies, but negatively affected by the shift of the price of goods.

price level, this may bias our results somewhat in favour of a lengthy classical unemployment.

As long as i_t remains negative (and $i_\tau < 0$ for $\tau = 2, 3, \ldots, t-1$), the unemployment rate is increasing and positive. Moreover v_{t-1} must be positive. Hence:

$$z_t \geqq (r'_w - a)v_{t-1} + (\beta L - s - \sigma r'_w)u_{t-1} \qquad (52)$$

must be positive, because we have assumed $r'_w > a$ and we may take it that σ is small enough to make $\beta L - s > \sigma r'_w$ (such a hypothesis will be considered again more closely at the beginning of the next chapter).

But v_t keeps decreasing and eventually becomes negative, forcing net investment to become positive.

Suppose now that the solution of system (51) leads to $i_t > 0$. We may understand that z_t is then bounded above by a number that would tend to zero if the unemployment rate would itself tend to zero. Hence, except for pathological cases, we may conclude that z_t will become negative before u_t.

When $r'_m = 0$, equation (50) and system (51) imply:

$$z_t \leqq (r'_w - a)v_{t-1} + (\beta L - s)u_t + \qquad (53)$$
$$+ (b\beta L - \sigma r'_w)u_{t-1}$$

But $i_t > 0$ requires $av_{t-1} < b\beta L u_{t-1}$; hence:

$$z_t < r'_w \left(\frac{b\beta L}{a} - \sigma \right) u_{t-1} + (\beta L - s)u_t \qquad (54)$$

The right-hand side of this inequality would clearly tend to zero if u_t would itself tend to zero.

Moreover, as long as classical unemployment prevails, the real wage keeps decreasing and the unemployment rate u_t given by (51) cannot remain positive for ever. Indeed, $i_t > -av_{t-1}$; hence $u_t - u_{t-1} < a\gamma v_{t-2}/\beta L$; as soon as the right-hand side of this inequality has become negative, u_t decreases at an increasing speed.

The preceding argument can be supported by a study of the

continuous process that would be derived from (50)–(51) if the elementary period were not equal to 1 but were infinitesimally small. Again neglecting real wealth effects, the system would then be:

$$z = r'_w v + (\beta L - s)u + i$$
$$i = -av + b \, \text{Min}(z, \beta L u)$$
$$\dot{u} = -\frac{\gamma}{\beta L} i \tag{55}$$
$$\dot{v} = \sigma u$$

in which $\dot{u}$ and $\dot{v}$ are the time derivatives of u and v.

This system has two regimes corresponding respectively to $z < \beta L u$ and $z > \beta L u$. One may see that each one of them essentially obeys a second order linear differential equation whose solution is a damped oscillation, unless σ is very small, i.e. unless the real wage rate is insensitive to classical unemployment, which may be ruled out. One may moreover see that, in both regimes, $z < 0$ when a shift from $u > 0$ to $u < 0$ occurs.

Hence, in the evolution following from (55), the initial positive bulge in z ends before the initial positive bulge in u and this occurs in finite time.

Considering the regime that would apply with $\beta L u < z$ will suffice here, since the other regime can be dealt with in the same manner. One may derive from (55) the following second order differential equation in u:

$$\ddot{u} + \gamma b \dot{u} + \frac{\gamma a \sigma}{\beta L} u = 0 \tag{56}$$

The two characteristic roots have negative real parts. They also have an imaginary part if:

$$\frac{\sigma}{\beta} > \gamma b \frac{bL}{4a} \tag{57}$$

In the right-hand side of this inequality, γb is smaller than 1 since the immediate adaptation of investment to capacity needs is only partial; the ratio $bL/4a$ is all the more small as investment is relatively more sensitive to profitability.

Considering that the solution of (56) is indeed a damped oscillation, we see that $u = 0$ and $\dot{u} < 0$ imply in this regime: $i > 0$ (since i and $\dot{u}$ have opposite signs) and $v < 0$ (since $i = -av + b\beta Lu$); moreover $i = -av$, hence $z = (r'_w - a)v$, which is negative; z is therefore already negative when v becomes negative, as we had to show.

To conclude this formal discussion, we may say that classical unemployment is most likely to end up as Keynesian unemployment. But, unless the adjustment of the price of goods is very fast and unless real balance effects are strong, this will not occur before the real wage rate has been forced down enough to make net investment (temporarily) positive, households' consumption being then quite depressed.

4 Some numerical experiments and the medium-term consequences of economic policies

The formal study of the dynamic properties of our system cannot be fully conclusive because of its difficulty. If we want to learn something from this system we must therefore be more specific. In particular numerical simulations will help us to reach a more concrete view of the type of description following from the preceding ideas.

An attempt will be made here to make these simulations relevant to actual situations. To this end, the full specification will aim at using realistic values for the parameters, even though the system is of course too simple to provide an accurate representation of the actual phenomena, which are indeed complex.

Numerical values of the parameters

In choosing a specification it will be proper to view the unit period as being something like a year. Indeed, in the system of the preceding chapter, the investment of one period depends on the economic situation during the preceding period and affects the productive capacity of the next period. These lags play an essential role in some of the dynamic characteristics of the system, in particular the length of spells of classical unemployment, which is of particular interest here. They certainly cannot be considered as shorter than a year on the average.

Some of the numerical values are inessential and depend on the choice of units of measurement. Hence, the labour supply will be taken to be $L = 1,000$ and labour productivity to be $\beta = 1$. Full employment output will then be equal to 1,000.

No lag has been introduced in the consumption function, except through the accumulation of savings and by real wealth effects. This being granted, we shall take a specification that should not raise major objections, namely:

$$c_t = 900w_t + 0.1m_t - 500u_t \tag{1}$$

This is admittedly a simple relation. It does not contain net transfer income h as an argument, but in the simulations we shall systematically assume this income flow to be zero.[1] The marginal propensity to consume is 0.1 out of real wealth, 0.9 out of full employment real labour income and something like 0.55 out of the variations of labour income resulting from variations in employment (we shall see that the 'appropriate' value of the real wage rate is taken to be 0.9 in most simulations). Various microeconomic justifications can be given for the existence of these three distinct propensities and for their ranking.

We shall take the capital–output ratio to be 2 and therefore γ to be 0.5.

Since the variations of the price level P play a role only through real wealth effects that cannot be taken as large, we shall not spend much time in discussing the equations explaining the changes of this price level. They will be taken as:

$$1,000\frac{P_{t+1} - P_t}{P_t} = (d_t - y_t) - 0.1(\beta L - y_t) \tag{2}$$

when classical unemployment prevails;

[1] If h is taken as constant and if it enters linearly into the consumption function, only inessential changes result in the following simulations.

$$1,000\frac{P_{t+1}-P_t}{P_t} = (d_t-y_t)+0.5(\bar{y}_t-\beta L) \qquad (3)$$

in the case of inflation; and

$$1,000\frac{P_{t+1}-P_t}{P_t} = -0.2(\bar{y}_t-y_t)-0.1((\beta L-y_t)(4)$$

when Keynesian unemployment holds.

Thus, the sensitivity to excess demand is taken to be five times larger than the sensitivity to excess supply.[2]

Two specifications are likely to play a very significant role in the present context: those concerning the spontaneous real wage rate changes and the investment function. They must be chosen with particular care, all the more so since the best numerical values are not obvious.

In chapter 3 we assumed that the real wage remains stable under Keynesian unemployment, but decreases under classical unemployment and increases under inflation. In the two latter cases the following equations will be taken for most simulations:

$$w_{t+1} = w_t - 0.2u_t \qquad (5)$$

when classical unemployment prevails;

$$w_{t+1} = w_t + 0.2\frac{\text{Min}(d_t,\bar{y}_t)-\beta L}{1,000} \qquad (6)$$

when inflation prevails.

According to (5) and (6) a 5 per cent change in the rate of excess supply or excess demand of labour induces a change of roughly 1.1 per cent in the annual rate of change of real wages. Although this order of magnitude agrees with the one

[2] It will be noted that equations (3) and (4) are respectively simpler than equations (24) and (25) of chapter 3 in which $\bar{y}_t$ is replaced respectively by $\text{Min}(d_t,\bar{y}_t)$ and by $\text{Min}(\bar{y}_t,\beta L)$. Considering that the revisions of the price level play only a minor role, one may see that the simplification is worth making.

occurring in some of the present macroeconometric models, it may be found somewhat too small by some critics. Hence, some simulations have been run in which 0.2 has been replaced by 0.5 in both (5) and (6).

Three positive parameters occur in the investment equations a, b and e. The last one is really inessential from the present point of view, because it affects mainly the characteristics of the Walrasian stationary equilibrium and only very slightly the dynamic process away from this equilibrium.

For simplicity e has been taken as equal to 0.1 in most simulations. Let us note, however, that this has two consequences for the Walrasian stationary equilibrium. Firstly, equation (21) of chapter 2 implies that government demand g be then equal to 100 (as soon as $h = \pi = 0$), which creates no difficulty. Secondly, equation (17) of the same chapter implies that the real net rate of return on capital is then equal to 20 per cent, which is admittedly too high. In order to check that the choice of e was really inessential, some simulations were run with $e = 0.02$, $g = 20$ and a real net rate of return on capital of 4 per cent.

The choice of the values of a and b is more delicate. On the one hand, we assumed $a < r'_w$, which means here that a must be smaller than 900. On the other hand, we do not want a to be too small, since our aim is here to explore the consequences of a direct relationship between profitability and investment. But existing econometric studies do not give a precise measure of this relationship. The parameter a has been taken as equal to 400 in most simulations; a 1 per cent change in the real labour cost (i.e. a 2 per cent change of the rate of return on capital) directly induces a change of 4 in annual net investment, i.e. a change of roughly 0.4 per cent per annum in the productive capacity. The value $a = 800$ was also used in some simulations.

As for b, the accelerator coefficient, it depends on how fast a perceived lack of capacity, $d_{t-1} - \bar{y}_{t-1}$ or $\beta L - \bar{y}_{t-1}$, is corrected by investment. The value $b = 0.25$ was used in most simulations, with $b = 0.5$ being tried in some of them.

When $e = 0.1$ and $g = 100$, the Walrasian stationary equilibrium is given by the following values of the real variables:

$$\left. \begin{array}{l} w = 0.9 \quad i = 0 \quad y = \bar{y} = \beta L = d = 1{,}000 \\ c = 900 \quad u = 0 \quad m = 900 \end{array} \right\} \quad (7)$$

When $e = 0.02$ and $g = 20$, the above values must be changed to:

$$\left. \begin{array}{l} w = 0.98 \quad i = 0 \quad y = \bar{y} = \beta L = d = 1{,}000 \\ c = 980 \quad u = 0 \quad m = 980 \end{array} \right\} \quad (8)$$

The spontaneous evolution from a too high wage rate

In order to consider the main results of the simulations we shall start from the point where we stopped at the end of the last chapter in our formal study of the dynamic process. Hence we shall consider the spontaneous evolution following from an initial situation $(t = 0)$ in which all real variables have the values corresponding to the Walrasian stationary equilibrium except that the real wage rate experiences (at $t = 1$) a sudden exogenous rise. No other shock will be assumed to occur either at this initial stage or later on.

In other words all the values will be given by (7) at $t = 0$; but at time $t = 1$ equation (5) will not apply and will actually be replaced by:

$$w_1 = 0.95 \tag{9}$$

Except for this, the system will be ruled by the equations given above with the parameter values that were specified to apply in 'most simulations' (in particular $\sigma = 0.2$, $e = 0.1$, $a = 400$, $b = 0.25$).

After having closely considered this particular evolution, we shall proceed to a sensitivity analysis in order to see how much its features depend on the values assumed for the various parameters.

Figure 3 presents the time path obtained after a sudden exogenous rise in the real wage rate. It gives visual support to the conclusions reached at the end of the last chapter. Net investment is negative from $t = 2$ to $t = 8$. It becomes positive at $t = 9$, when the real wage has lost more than half of its exogenous advance and when the pressure of excess demand on capacity is strong (at $t = 8$, $d_t - \bar{y}_t = 40$). In the initial phase of classical unemployment, the unemployment rate rises to a level exceeding 4 per cent and remains roughly constant from $t = 8$ to $t = 14$. The real wage rate then steadily decreases and becomes smaller than its appropriate level after $t = 10$. The rate of increase that is imposed by excess demand on the price level is 2.5 per cent during period 1; it rises to 3.9 per cent for $t = 6$ and then decreases.

At period $t = 14$ Keynesian unemployment appears and then develops its course. Investment becomes negative again after $t = 19$. The unemployment rate rises again steadily. But the movement towards the Keynesian unemployment stationary equilibrium is rather slow. At $t = 50$ the following values obtain:[3]

$\bar{y} = 951$, $y = 899$, $u = 10.1$ per cent. But the stationary equilibrium corresponds to: $\bar{y} = 909$, $y = 864$, $u = 15.6$ per cent. The reason for this rather slow movement is apparent from figure 3: the shift of real wealth to its equilibrium level is very slow; at $t = 50$ we find $m = 667$ whereas the equilibrium value is $m = 472$. To be complete, let us still note that at the 'stationary' Keynesian equilibrium the rate of decrease of the price level is 2.5 per cent per period.

Of all the features of this simulation the rather considerable

---

[3] Let us remember that the model does not claim to represent long-term phenomena. If the simulations were run up to $t = 50$ it was in order to permit a good grasp of the properties of the model and not to represent the actual spontaneous long-term consequences of the hypotheses adopted for the initial situation.

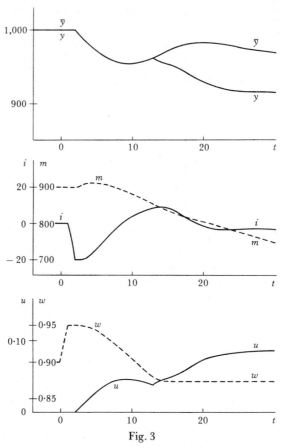

Fig. 3

length of the spell of classical unemployment has particular interest. Sensitivity analysis is particularly needed in this respect. It confirms that this length is somewhat reduced if higher values of a or σ are used, but that changes of b or e do not really matter for it.

A simulation was run with $a = 800$ instead of $a = 400$, all other parameters keeping the values used for figure 3. This corresponds to an increased impact of profitability on investment. Keynesian unemployment appears for $t = 12$ instead of $t = 14$. The real wage is then down to $w = 0.828$ instead of $w = 0.872$, because classical unemployment is much more severe, with the rate of unemployment reaching a maximum of 9 per cent for $t = 8$ and 9.

Another simulation was run with $b = 0.5$ instead of $b = 0.25$, all other parameters including a having the same values as for figure 3. This corresponds to an increased role for pressure on capacity in the demand for investment.[4] Keynesian unemployment appears for $t = 15$ instead of $t = 14$. But unemployment is lower, both in the initial classical phase and in the subsequent Keynesian phase; this results from the fact that net investment becomes positive sooner ($t = 7$ instead of $t = 9$). After a maximum of 3.4 per cent at $t = 7$ the unemployment rate decreases to 0.6 per cent when Keynesian unemployment appears (with $w = 0.892$ instead of $w = 0.872$). It then rises to a maximum of 4.7 per cent for $t = 21$; the maximum excess capacity is equal to 33 and occurs at $t = 20$. With such a high value of b, the Keynesian stationary equilibrium is no longer stable because inequality (48) of chapter 3 no longer applies ($\gamma = 0.5$ and $k = 2$). This appears in the simulation when new classical phases occur: at $t = 24$, 25, lowering the real wage rate to $w = 0.879$, at $t = 37$, 38, lowering it to $w = 0.847$, at $t = 48$ and again at $t = 50, \ldots$ Hence eventually the unemployment rate becomes very high and the whole process diverges. Except for this particularity, which is fairly slow to appear, the change in the value of b does not affect the shapes of the time paths described in figure 3, but makes them less unfavourable.

In the simulation corresponding to a high sensitivity of the real wage rate to classical unemployment ($\sigma = 0.5$ instead of $\sigma = 0.2$), the initial classical spell is shorter of course; but it still lasts up to $t = 8$ (instead of $t = 13$). The real wage rate is

[4] This value $b = 0.5$ is high. Indeed, if lags are neglected, the Keynesian multiplier becomes infinite in this case, because the derivative of consumption and investment with respect to output are both equal to 0.5.

lowered to $w = 0.864$ instead of $w = 0.872$. The unemployment rate is somewhat higher all the way through the Keynesian phase. But the evolutions are very similar to those of figure 3.

Finally the simulation run with $e = 0.02$ and $g = 20$ (instead of $e = 0.1$ and $g = 100$) confirmed that the choice of e was almost inessential. The shift from classical to Keynesian unemployment occurred for $t = 13$ instead of $t = 14$. The discrepancy $\beta - e - w$ then rose to 0.022 instead of 0.028. The unemployment rate remained almost the same up to $t = 35$; it then rose a little faster (for $t = 50$, $u = 11.0$ instead of $u = 10.1$ per cent).

Other spontaneous evolutions

The preceding section provided a rather close scrutiny of the dynamics of classical unemployment following from an initial situation in which the real wage rate was too high. We must now consider more quickly the time paths that follow from other initial situations. For these simulations we keep the same values of the parameters as for figure 3 (in particular $\sigma = 0.2$, $e = 0.1$, $a = 400$, $b = 0.25$).

It is not necessary now to spend time considering what would happen if the initial situation differed from the Walrasian stationary equilibrium only by too low a wage rate. Notwithstanding some temporary stimulus given to investment, a Keynesian unemployment results and it develops almost exactly as in the second part of the simulation of the preceding section. Unemployment rises progressively, output decreases, with an excess productive capacity that reaches a maximum at $t = 6$. The movement to the Keynesian stationary equilibrium is slow with a continuous decline in real wealth.

In order to consider the consequences of too low an aggregate demand we may look at a simulation in which the initial values are those of the Walrasian equilibrium except that the real wealth is too small:[5] $m = 600$ instead of $m = 900$. A situation of Keynesian unemployment results, with the unemployment rate reaching $u = 9.8$ per cent for $t = 3$ and $t = 4$, net investment then being equal to -22. Later on the accelerator is less strong whereas real wealth slowly increases. Hence the unemployment rate decreases. But a lack of productive capacity occurs at $t = 9$, the unemployment then becoming classical with $u = 5.6$ per cent. This new situation depresses the real wage from $w = 0.90$ to $w = 0.89$. This is enough to make unemployment Keynesian again. From then on the time path slowly converges to the Keynesian stationary equilibrium corresponding to $w = 0.89$, the only qualitative difference from the two previously considered cases being that the equilibrium is here approached 'from below': output, capacity and real wealth slowly increase.

The symmetrical situation may be examined, in which a sudden exogenous increase of real wealth occurs in the Walrasian stationary equilibrium ($m = 1,200$ instead of $m = 900$, for instance as a consequence of large and exceptional transfer payments to consumers). It is somewhat special because, with the behaviour relations that have been assumed, the excess demand for goods has no impact on the demand for labour. The firms are producing at full capacity and are therefore not looking for more labour. On the other

[5] This particular situation may be viewed as resulting from an exceptional levy on consumers' assets. But this is inessential; the main point is that aggregate demand is depressed in the initial period and later on, as long as real assets have not been restored to their level in the Walrasian stationary equilibrium. Another simulation was run with $m_1 = 900$ but $g = 70$ for all t instead of $g = 100$, so that the initial depression of aggregate demand is the same. But interpretation of this alternative simulation is not easy, because the values of the exogenous variables are then inconsistent with the existence of a Walrasian stationary equilibrium (the income flows cannot be in equilibrium because equation (23) of chapter 2 is not fulfilled). One may even check that no Keynesian stationary equilibrium exists either. Let us note, however, that the resulting Keynesian unemployment develops continuously according to an increasing trend, except for an initial bulge ($u = 11.9$ at $t = 5$, 10.5 at $t = 10$, 12.5 at $t = 20$, 18.2 at $t = 50$, with $w = 0.90$ all the way through).

hand profitability remains at its appropriate level and the excess demand for goods does not stimulate investment because no more labour is available; hence, net investment remains equal to zero. The only difference from the Walrasian stationary equilibrium is that the excess demand for goods induces an increase of the price level and thus a decrease of real wealth. The rate of increase of prices is initially 3 per cent per period, but progressively decreases; it is smaller than 1 per cent after $t = 10$, while the real wealth has become smaller than 1,000. This time path, which progressively leads back to the Walrasian stationary equilibrium, follows from a sequence of temporary equilibria that are intermediate between inflation and classical unemployment, the labour market being always just cleared.

The case in which initial productive capacity is too small in comparison with the labour supply and the demand for goods is not interesting at this stage, because it brings us back to the consideration of classical unemployment that was studied in the preceding section. The reverse case is more interesting, in which productive capacity is too large (for instance $\bar{y} = 1,100$) whereas all other variables have initially the values corresponding to the Walrasian stationary equilibrium. This is another case in which this Walrasian equilibrium tends to be restored through a sequence of temporary equilibria; these are here characterized by Keynesian unemployment. Indeed, net investment is initially depressed ($i = -40$ for $t = 3$, with $u = 7.7$ per cent); as productive capacity is reduced, this effect becoming progressively smaller (for $t = 8$, $i = -7.7$ and $u = 1.4$ per cent). But in the present case the time path does *not* converge to the Walrasian stationary equilibrium. Indeed, in period $t = 9$ the productive capacity, $\bar{y} = 994$, becomes smaller than demand; from $t = 9$ to $t = 12$ unemployment is classical and induces a decrease of the real wage rate to $w = 0.895$; from then on unemployment becomes Keynesian again and the time path slowly converges to a Keynesian stationary equilibrium with $u = 1.9$ per cent; this is a rather small deviation from the Walrasian equilibrium considering the size of the initial disequilibrium.

More complex initial discrepancies from the Walrasian stationary equilibrium may also be considered. For instance a state of inflation will result if there is excess capacity and if autonomous demand is large enough. In particular, a simulation was run starting from the initial values $\bar{y}_0 = 1,100$ and $m_1 = 1,500$ (and also $w_0 = w_1 = 0.9, y_0 = 1,000$). There is then in period 1 an excess demand for goods equal to 35 and an excess demand for labour equal to the same amount. Inflation lasts until period $t = 11$, when productive capacity becomes smaller than full employment output; the excess demand for goods is then still equal to $z = 25$ and the real wage rate has increased to $w = 0.934$. Classical unemployment lasts from period $t = 11$ to period $t = 22$, and the real wage rate decreases to $w = 0.878$; the unemployment rate is then equal to $u = 2.2$ per cent, after a local maximum of $u = 3.0$ per cent in period $t = 17$. From then on, the by now familiar slow convergence to a Keynesian stationary state follows.[6]

It may also be interesting to consider *a simulation that would mimic the effect of the 'oil shock'*. This had a dual nature. On the one hand the previously prevailing real income rates in Western countries became inadequate because of the sudden shift in the terms of trade; in particular the real wage rates became too high. On the other hand a demand deficit

[6] In order to see whether inflation could not lead directly to the Keynesian equilibrium, some simulations were run in which the initial value of the real wage rate was low. None of them disproved the spontaneous sequence: inflation *to* classical unemployment *to* Keynesian unemployment. (A shift from inflation to Keynesian unemployment, however, occurred in a situation that was very close to the Walrasian stationary equilibrium and while the value $b = 0.5$ was used. The following values of the variables were then prevailing: $\bar{y} = 1,001, w = 0.899, m = 912$.) For instance a simulation started with the initial values $y_0 = 1,000$; $\bar{y}_0 = 1,020$; $w_0 = w_1 = 0.87$; $m_1 = 2,000$. Inflation lasted from $t = 1$ to $t = 13$, with net investment being first positive then negative; from $t = 14$, when the real wage was equal to $w = 0.924$, to $t = 25$, classical unemployment prevailed with the real wage ending at $w = 0.885$; then Keynesian unemployment held.

occurred because some of the major oil exporters were unable to spend all their export earnings. Hence, a simulation was run with $y_0 = \bar{y}_0 = 1,000$ but with $w_0 = w_1 = 0.93$ and $m = 600$. (The reason has previously been given as to why changes in autonomous demand are introduced here through changes in real wealth.)

The effect of this 'oil shock' is an initial spell of Keynesian unemployment with negative net investment.[7] This ends up in period $t = 5$ with insufficient productive capacity leading to classical unemployment, which lasts for five periods during which the real wage rate is depressed to $w = 0.885$; then unemployment is Keynesian again. The following values of the rate of unemployment are recorded (in per cent): $u_1 = 3.0$, $u_2 = 3.9$, $u_3 = 3.7$, $u_4 = 2.8$, $u_5 = 3.4$, $u_6 = 4.1$, $u_8 = 4.9$, $u_{10} = 5.6$, $u_{12} = 5.1$, $u_{15} = 5.4$, $u_{20} = 5.9$; the last one is almost equal to the value corresponding to the stationary Keynesian equilibrium.

Corrective policies

The simulations can also be used to exhibit the short- and medium-term consequences of economic policies if the model were a perfect description of the actual economic system. As was explained at the beginning of chapter 3, the policy measures must be understood as shocks that impose exogenous shifts to the spontaneous evolutions. We shall consider here mainly the question of how to cure the Keynesian depression, but we shall also examine briefly policies intended to deal with the oil shock.

The Keynesian depression, i.e. the situation that occurs along the slow convergence to a Keynesian stationary

---

[7] Assuming that the real wage rate remains constant throughout this initial spell, as our process does, may be particularly inappropriate. The excess supply on the goods market soon becomes small so that the depressing effect may be stronger on wages than on prices. Moreover the fact that real wages are too high may be recognized in wage bargains.

equilibrium, is characterized both by too low a real wage rate and by an excess productive capacity. Pure demand management can be used, as well as an incomes policy that raises the real wage rate.

In order to study these corrective policies let us assume an initial situation with an unemployment rate of 10 per cent ($y_0 = 900$), excess capacity of 5 per cent ($\bar{y}_0 = 950$), a real wage rate $w_0 = 0.87$ and real wealth $m_1 = 600$. In the absence of any corrective policy, the unemployment rate would rise to 11.5 per cent for $t = 1$ and, from $t = 2$ on, exceed 12 per cent.[8]

Demand management that could be represented as a pure transfer of wealth to consumers may be studied if we compare this situation with another one in which m_1 is higher. Two simulations were run with respectively $m_1 = 900$ and $m_1 = 800$. Both were, of course, successful in the short run with the unemployment rate reduced below 6 per cent during the first five periods when $m_1 = 900$ and below 6.6 per cent from $t = 2$ to $t = 5$, when $m_1 = 800$. But in the longer run these policies would not prevent the Keynesian depression from resuming its course. Moreover, too large an increase in demand appears to be dangerous because of the limitation on productive capacities: whereas with $m_1 = 800$ unemployment remains Keynesian, with $m_1 = 900$ a lack of capacity appears at $t = 2$ depressing the real wage rate to $w = 0.86$ and therefore permanently reducing aggregate demand; from $t = 8$ on, the unemployment rate is larger with the simulation originating with $m_1 = 900$ than from the one originating with $m_1 = 800$. For the latter it amounts to 8.0 per cent at $t = 8$, to 9.9 per cent at $t = 20$ and to 11.8 at $t = 50$.

For the study of a pure incomes policy acting on the real

---

[8] Actually it would have been better for these simulations to take an initial situation of $m_1 = 675$ (and $y_0 = 900$, $\bar{y}_0 = 950$, $w_0 = 0.87$), because the unemployment rate would then have increased only very slowly from its initial level of 10 per cent. This alternative initial situation may be kept in mind when studying pure demand management policies.

wage rate,[9] two simulations were run with an exogenous rise in the real wage at $t = 1$ and respectively $w_1 = 0.90$ and $w_1 = 0.92$ (while $y_0 = 900, \bar{y}_0 = 950, m_1 = 600$). Except for the two first periods, the results of the two simulations are very similar: indeed with $w_1 = 0.92$ demand exceeds productive capacity which lowers the real wage rate, so that $w = 0.90$ for $t = 3$, 4 and 5 in both simulations. The only significant difference is therefore for u_1 and u_2 which are roughly equal to 6 per cent when $w_1 = 0.90$ and to 5 per cent when $w_1 = 0.92$. But lack of capacity is not avoided later on; it appears at $t = 6$ with $w_1 = 0.90$ and it appears again at $t = 5$ with $w_1 = 0.92$; in both cases the real wage rate falls to $w = 0.889$, which of course is more favourable than the previous $w = 0.87$ but explains why permanent unemployment is not completely removed (the unemployment rate decreases very slowly from 7 per cent, after the reduction of the real wage rate, to 6 per cent for $t = 18$ and to 5 per cent for $t = 50$). Some excess capacity exists, however, which would permit a new small exogenous rise either in autonomous demand or in real wages (excess capacity is equal to 10 for $t = 9$ and slowly increases thereafter to 16 for $t = 50$).

Comparison between the two types of policy shows that they have similar effects in the short run (the first few periods), but that attempts at restoring the appropriate income distribution are more successful than pure demand management policies in the medium run for curing unemployment. This is, of course, a very crude comparison. Many strategies can be defined in which economic policy may use a sequence of exogenous actions of various types; some of these strategies will dominate those resulting from a once and for all action. But the purpose

[9] We suppose here that measures are found that have the combined result of raising the wage rate while leaving the price level unchanged. If the policy is to raise the real wage rate and to accept an induced change in the price level, the shock will affect not only w but also m. Its consequences may be understood from what is learnt here about demand management on the one hand and about a 'pure' incomes policy on the other hand.

of the theoretical model discussed here cannot be to define such optimal strategies.

No simulation was actually run for dealing with the 'oil shock', i.e. with a situation in which demand is deficient but, at the same time the real wage rate is too high. But it is quite clear that in this situation a rise in the real wage rate, which would help in the short run, would make the medium-term problem still more acute. Demand management is required as a complement to an incomes policy that is intended to reduce the real wage rate. The combination of the proper dose of demand stimulation with the proper action for wage restraint is of course difficult to find in practice. But the model clearly shows a rationale for the policies recently followed by several Western governments.

The conclusion of these simulations is more generally to support the importance that practitioners attribute to incomes policies intended to correct deviations that have occurred from the appropriate income distribution.

It would have been futile to run many more such simulations since the model does not claim precisely to represent any actual economy. For a persuasive study of economic policies good macroeconometric models must of course be used; and this is now a familiar exercise.

It is, however, interesting to note that even a model built on very crude hypotheses can produce suggestive results. In particular the theoretical model being discussed here seems to come closer to actual econometric models than do those elaborated either by the theory of business fluctuations or by the theory of growth.

5 Aggregation, expectations, finance and substitutions

In the three preceding chapters the argument relied on a very simple model, thanks to which some important macro-economic relationships could be easily visualized. The solution of the model was interpreted as relevant for an understanding of actual phenomena involving unemployment. But the great limitations of the model should be kept in mind. The risk is quite real that this model gives a biassed representation of the facts. Hence, we must proceed to a heuristic reexamination of the previous conclusions in order to see how they have to be changed when a more faithful representation of the world is considered.

We should pay particular attention to what appear at this stage as the two major claims of this book: on the one hand that the study of macroeconomic policies and of their medium-term consequences should take the distribution of incomes and its effect on profitability into account, and on the other hand that classical unemployment, although not stable, may, if it occurs, last longer than has been thought, because the corrective reduction of real wage rates and the rebuilding of productive capacities both require time.

Four features of the model require reexamination because they are at variance with reality as we now see it: (i) the model is fully aggregated whereas one observes a great variety of situations coexisting at the same time in the same country, (ii) expectations have been taken as essentially exogenous whereas they actually depend on previously experienced economic evolution, (iii) although the consistency of the model with respect to the balancing of income and financial flows has been considered, no real attention has been paid to the financial constraints that slow down investment in some circumstances, and (iv) the assumption of strict complementarity between capital and labour neglects possibilities of substitution that certainly play a role in the medium run.

Sectoral unemployment

When one thinks about classical unemployment, it is hard to believe that it could apply simultaneously in all industries and all regions, because casual observation does not seem to reveal the existence of such a situation at any time. On the other hand, 'pockets' of classical unemployment have often been identified, namely cases in which the productive capacity is not there to make some goods that are demanded and to employ a labour force that is willing and able to work on this production. The real question is to know how important such cases are and whether they tend, at any time, to become more or less frequent.

The theoretical analysis should therefore not rely only on an aggregated model but also consider how intersectoral disparities affect the phenomena under study. It is intuitively clear that such disparities stimulate intersectoral mobility, as well as changes in relative prices. The dynamics of the phenomena are therefore likely to be significantly different from those of a totally aggregated analysis: one may be sure that the evolution is smoother; one may also guess that the added flexibility does stabilize the system and makes imbalance less serious.

Indeed, we are here touching a difficulty that faces any attempt at using economic theories for looking at the real world: macroeconomic theories stress contradictions whereas microeconomic theories see adaptations everywhere; truth is somewhere in between.

It is not difficult in the present case to define the framework of a disaggregated model, but hardly feasible to deal with it precisely.[1]

Let us suppose that the sectorization simultaneously concerns the labour force, the productive capacity and the demand for goods. In other words, at any given time a sector has a certain amount of equipment available, faces a well specified and specific labour supply, as well as a specific demand for its products. This is certainly an extreme and simplifying hypothesis, but it does provide a useful approximation for the short run if a sector is understood as meaning one industry in one region.

If there are n such sectors (n being the number of industries multiplied by the number of regions), if a particular sector is denoted as j, then we may speak of its labour force L_j, of its productive capacity $\bar{y}_j$, of the productivity β_j that it achieves and of the demand d_j for its product. We may moreover assume the following relation for the determination of its output:

$$y_j = \text{Min}\{\beta_j L_j, \bar{y}_j, d_j\} \qquad (1)$$

At any time the demand d_j depends on the situation in the whole economy; it depends for instance on the overall unemployment rate. Once this relationship has been specified, which raises no fundamental difficulty, a model of short-run equilibrium is available. For any equilibrium it is possible to say which sectors respectively are in an inflationary, classical or Keynesian situation. It is also possible to define the respective weights P_I, P_C and P_K of these three situations, for instance by considering the intersectoral distribution of the labour force $(P_I + P_C + P_K = 1)$. With respect to such a disaggregated model, we may say that the short-term equilibria studied in chapter 3 correspond to the three extreme cases $P_I = 1$, $P_C = 1$ and $P_K = 1$. We may guess that intermediate cases have intermediate properties.

---

[1] The static disaggregated model is studied in my article 'Macroeconomic rationing of employment' in J. P. Fitoussi and E. Malinvaud, ed., *Unemployment in Western societies*, Macmillan, London 1980.

For the present dynamic study, the difficulty is to describe correctly how, through time and as a consequence of the actual evolution, the intersectoral distribution of the labour force, the intersectoral distribution of the demand for goods and the productive capacities of the various sectors change. These changes are stimulated by the imbalances in the various markets, as well as by intersectoral disparities in prices and profitability. Such imbalances and disparities simultaneously change as a consequence of shifts in the distributions of the supply of labour and demand for goods.

Without attempting a full analysis of these complex interdependences, we may however see why the aggregate model is likely to convey too pessimistic a view about the operation of the economy. Let us assume for instance that deterioration of profitability has been responsible for some classical unemployment $(P_C > 0)$, but not for a situation of generalized classical unemployment $(P_C < 1)$ since we believe that such an extreme situation is not likely to be observed. One would get too pessimistic a view of the subsequent evolution if one isolated the sectors experiencing classical unemployment and described their dynamic behaviour by applying to them the aggregate analysis of chapter 4.

To make the argument a little more precise, but still very heuristic, let us consider the case in which there was unemployment in all sectors but half of it was classical and half Keynesian $(P_C = P_K = 0.5)$. Let us moreover assume that the same wage rate prevails in all sectors (this property may be a good approximation in economies where social forces rather than market forces tend to determine it). There is then no particular incentive for labour to move from one sector to another. But there are reasons for shifts in the demand for goods and for changes in relative prices.

On the one hand, part of the demand that cannot be fulfilled during the current period by sectors experiencing a classical situation will be transferred in the next period to sectors experiencing a Keynesian situation. One may intuitively understand that this will be a factor causing a reduction of unemployment, because Keynesian sectors will expand production while classical sectors will still work at full capacity.

On the other hand, the pressure of demand for goods will tend to push prices up in the classical sectors and down in the Keynesian ones. It is, however, difficult to know whether the change in relative prices between the two groups of sectors will be larger or smaller in the real world of interacting sectors than in an abstract model in which the two groups were isolated from one another, each one operating according to the process presented in chapter 3. (Indeed, in this model relative prices would also change in favour of the goods produced by the classical sectors, even after correction for the different rates of increase of nominal wages.) For one thing, intersectoral shifts in the demand for goods will relieve part of the pressure that pushes prices up in classical sectors and down in Keynesian ones. But we must also realize that the price–wage spiral is likely to play little role in the disaggregated model, whereas it would slow down the correction of real wages in the submodel that would apply to classical sectors if these were considered in isolation; in other words, social forces are likely to be much less effective in blocking the restoration of profitability if this restoration is limited to some sectors rather than affecting the whole economy.

All in all, we see a reason for the aggregate analysis of the preceding chapters to overestimate unemployment, as well as excess demand or excess supply for goods; but we see no clear evidence that would imply a bias in the representation previously given of the evolution of productive capacity in each type of situation. Hence, the fluctuations of the unemployment rate are likely to be smoother and less extreme; but we do not seem able to learn whether they will also be shorter or longer.

It may be worth noting at this stage that viewing demand and supply in sectoral terms is also useful when international trade is taken into account. In the short run the level of demand in a particular country can be considered as given; in the medium run it shifts, depending in particular on international changes in relative prices, as well as on excess demand or supply at home and abroad.[2]

Endogenous expectations

It has always been recognized that expectations play a great role in shaping business fluctuations. They are moreover at the heart of the present analysis since the relationship between profitability and investment depends on the fact that the future is uncertain; this relationship therefore directly depends on the state of expectations.

It would be quite in order to argue here that changes in expectations react on the whole range of phenomena that have been explored in this book and to argue that such changes have therefore to be introduced whenever they occur. Any attempt at applying the present analysis should also start by a study of expectations, in the same way as does any attempt at applying a purely Keynesian analysis.

But such an argument does not do justice to the problem since this book aims at looking beyond the short run, for which expectations can usually be taken as given.[3] The real difficulty

---

[2] It has been argued that a small open economy can experience only classical and not Keynesian unemployment (see A. Dixit, 'The Balance of Trade in a Model of Temporary Equilibrium with Rationing', *Review of Economic Studies*, October 1978). I consider this argument as misleading because it relies on two usually unwarranted hypotheses: (i) that the foreign market is one of excess demand for goods, (ii) that this excess demand is instantaneously transmitted to the domestic market. It is true that the international market for goods tends to impose its features on the domestic market of a small open country, but this tendency may require some time to be effective; moreover it may lead toward Keynesian unemployment as well as toward inflation or classical unemployment.

[3] Nowadays this statement is disputed and one must indeed remember that dramatic changes of economic policy have, even in the short run, an impact on expectations. But it would not be realistic to consider such dramatic changes as frequent. For the range of policies that are usually under discussion it is a quite admissible approximation to take expectations as exogenous in the short run.

comes from the fact that expectations react to the economic evolution, so that their induced changes ought to be taken into account when either the spontaneous economic evolution or the various evolutions following from different policy strategies are being studied. In this respect the present book is particularly weak. Reflexion on the consequences of such a state of affairs is in order at this late stage.

A satisfactory treatment of the determination of expectations is not easy to find. Indeed, this conclusion follows from a study of the recent theoretical work about 'rational expectations'. Considering briefly this work will help to understand the issue.

The principle that leads to the definition and study of rational expectations is certainly a sound one, namely the request that the formalization of expectations imposes consistency with the environment in the same way as does the formalization of any other behaviour. In the same way as a rational consumer does not ignore his budget constraint, a rational agent does not ignore, when forming his expectations, the information he has about the economy, its past and its likely future course.

The consequences of this principle are clear enough in two cases. Firstly, when one considers the theory of long-term growth and therefore focuses attention on some very regular evolutions, one must recognize that agents living through these evolutions will have learned their characteristics, in one way or another. Agents will therefore hold correct or 'self-fulfilling' expectations. For instance if the price level grows by a fixed factor of $1+\pi$ every year, agents will expect it to grow by precisely this factor; they will therefore choose their behaviour taking this correct expectation into account. If two distinct long-term policy strategies are being compared and if the respective resulting rates of inflation are going to be π_1 and π_2, then account must be taken of the fact that agents will hold correct expectations in both cases; their behaviour will be consistent with an inflation rate of π_1 in the first case, of π_2 in the second case. Notice in passing, however, that this rule does not imply that the choice between the two strategies matters less than if the same expectations were held in both cases. No logical link *a priori* exists between the correctness of expectations and the ineffectiveness of (long-term) economic policies. Those who hold that such a link exists must prove it.

Secondly, theories of economic organization, including in particular theories of equilibrium for markets in which uncertainty plays a large role, have to model not only the environment as well as individual behaviour and expectations, but also how information reaches each agent. The situations considered are fundamentally complex but are again studied from the point of view of their long-term consequences. Theoretical research must then take advantage of the properties resulting from the usually valid assumption that expectations will rationally follow from the information the agents will receive about the environment. In some cases these properties may even be directly assumed without a full specification of the information structure and of the learning process, the latter being part of individual behaviour. The hypothesis of 'rational expectations' is then a particularly powerful device for circumventing some of the complexities of the problem.

But it is doubtful whether the hypotheses that are appropriate for expectations in growth models or in theories of economic organization can usefully be transposed when the medium-term dynamics of business fluctuations are being considered. It is then certainly not appropriate to assume that at all times correct expectations prevail, i.e. that agents figure out exactly what the current state of the economy is and its spontaneous subsequent evolution, not to speak of subsequent changes of economic policy or of other exogenous factors. The study of medium-term dynamics is bound to use more 'ad hoc', but also more valid, arguments.

What is to be attempted at this stage in this book must remain modest. The main question is to know which modifications to the analysis of the previous chapters ought to follow from the fact that agents progressively learn about their environment. Three such modifications seem to be worth considering. Two of them should mainly concern the Keynesian depression, since it is the only stable situation; but they may also play a role when inflation or classical unemployment prevails.

Uncertainty as to future demand (and future labour supply) was an essential factor in the justification of the investment function used here. It was assumed in section 3 of chapter 2 that firms have a (subjective) probability distribution F concerning the future minimum $\hat{y}$ of d and βL; it was also assumed that F is subject to shifts and that its position depends on the observed value of $\hat{y}$. The function F represents precisely some of the expectations held by firms and its supposed shifts provide a crude representation of the fact that firms adapt their expectations on the basis of what they observe.

But it should appear at this stage that the representation is too crude if it is intended to be kept unchanged for a rather long series of periods and despite the situations experienced during this series. In particular if there was convergence toward a stationary state, then it should be admitted that expectations become increasingly precise during this process. In other words, the distribution F should become increasingly concentrated. Neglect of this tendency explains why a Keynesian stationary state has been found in which a constant and positive excess capacity was maintained; this is paradoxical, since in a stationary state this excess capacity serves no purpose; it could exist only if firms did not realize that the economy had become stationary.

Revising the model in this respect would, however, not make the Keynesian depression look any more rosy. It would indeed mean that F would progressively become more concentrated, i.e. would increase for large values of $\hat{y}$ and decrease for small ones. But in the Keynesian depression the capacity $\bar{y}$ corresponds to a value of $\hat{y}$ that is high with respect to the average expected value, because the profit margin is favourable; this means that F would tend to increase for values of $\hat{y}$ in the neighbourhood of $\bar{y}$. Hence, the required capacity, $\bar{y}$, implied by formula (11) of chapter 2 for given values of y, w and q, would progressively decrease, as expectations became more and more accurate. This is an additional depressing factor. One may, however, check that, since the concentration of expectations is a slow process, it does not destroy the existence and stability of the Keynesian stationary state. (Actually, for a given value of w, the stationary state remains the same as in chapter 3, except for productive capacity.)

Expectations were also explicitly introduced in the model when the equations defining changes in the price level were specified. The rate of change was assumed to be the sum of two components, one depending on excess demand or supply, the other being 'the expected rate of inflation' π. The latter was moreover assumed to be exogenous and constant.

Whereas one can easily accept the notion that a two component formula of this type is a good macroeconomic approximation for a very complex phenomenon, one would have serious difficulties in accepting that the expected rate of inflation was constant, through time as well as between evolutions resulting from distinct policy strategies. Indeed, this latter assumption cannot be defended, as soon as the evolutions extend beyond a few successive periods.

At the very least, the component π ought to be replaced by a slowly evolving series that would to some extent reflect the rates of inflation during preceding periods. For some range of values of these rates, the alteration to the model would probably make the price series more volatile. For instance during a phase of inflation in which the real excess demand remained constant, one would find not a constant rate of inflation (as the model of chapters 3 and 4 assumes) but an increasing rate of inflation, i.e. a continuous acceleration of the rate of inflation.

But again it is doubtful whether the revision of the model

would substantially change the vision that has been offered here of the Keynesian depression. Considering present institutions it would be hard to believe in a model that would lead to a permanent increase in the rate of *decrease* of the price level. Hence, perhaps after a phase of rapid deceleration, the rate of inflation will be assumed to stabilize at a negative, or even perhaps at a positive,[4] value.

As soon as we note that the price equation should contain distributed lags because the expected rate of inflation depends on past inflation rates, we must recognize that more lags than were granted ought to be present also in other equations. For instance it might be argued that the real wage rate ought still to decrease in the initial periods of the Keynesian phase following a phase of classical unemployment, because of distributed lags in the formation of prices and wages. But such a revision of the basic model would not change its qualitative conclusions.

Similarly, one may wonder what role could be played by changes in consumers' expectations, which the model neglects too much. In chapter 2, consumers' behaviour was represented by the consumption function, which was directly assumed to depend only on the current real wage rate, real wealth and the unemployment rate. But it is clear that consumers' behaviour also depends on their expectations as to future real wages, the price level, the states of the labour and goods markets, and so on. If expectations change, the consumption function may have to change also. From the present point of view this remark should lead us to inquire as to how induced changes in expectations affect consumption.

Since induced changes in expectations are functions of past evolutions, their effect on consumers' behaviour can in principle be incorporated into the specification of the consumption function. For instance if we can assume that

---

[4] It was pure convenience that π was taken as zero in most of chapter 3 and we saw that assuming it to be positive would not have resulted in qualitatively different conclusions.

expectations on future real wages depend only on w_{t-1} and w_t, we may add $w_t - w_{t-1}$ as an argument of the consumption function; it will then be natural to assume that consumption is an increasing function not only of w_t but also of $w_t - w_{t-1}$. The same type of justification can be argued to make consumption decrease not only with the unemployment rate u_t but also with its variation $u_t - u_{t-1}$.

Introducing such distributed lags will again change somewhat the dynamics of the system, and probably in the direction of greater instability. But it will not change its main qualitative features and cannot in particular play a large role in the Keynesian depression.

Financial constraints

It may seem surprising that financial constraints are not really discussed in this book. Indeed, whereas the relationship between profitability and investment has been the central theme, no attention has been paid to the often heard proposition that profits are required in order to finance investment. Whereas business fluctuations were involved, during which financial conditions may vary greatly and affect behaviour, this component of the phenomena has not been considered. Whereas the logical approach would be to study equilibria under rationing constraints, an apparently important type of constraint has been systematically neglected.

The true reason for such a surprising feature is of course that this book does not claim to exhaust the theory of medium-term evolution. The main concern has been profitability as a precondition for risk taking by entrepreneurs; the model cannot do much more than explore the consequences of such a precondition. Others' will have to study the role of financial constraints.

In order to do so, they will have to disaggregate financial assets and probably distinguish at least three types of assets: equities, bonds and money. They will also have to look at public finance more precisely than has been done here. The existing literature suggests that the analysis will then be complex and that drawing synthetic conclusions from it will be difficult. Anticipating here the results that will be derived would be very risky indeed.

A modest objective may be, however, to search for cases in which even a purely aggregated examination would suggest the occurrence of financial tensions. But then only very provisional conclusions can follow because the identification of such tensions must rely on 'ad hoc' criteria whose validity cannot but be limited.

We know that, at the level of aggregation adopted here, the financial operations are in balance all along the sequence of temporary equilibria in all cases studied. Indeed, we checked the condition $M = M_f + M_g$, namely that the assets of consumers meet the financial requirements of firms and government. We know that this condition always holds and does not require any other market constraints than those explicitly introduced in the analysis concerning the goods and the labour markets.

But the evolution of M_f may, in conjunction with the evolution of other characteristics of business activity, suggest cases in which some difficulties might arise. For instance if M_f increases rapidly, i.e. if the global financial needs of firms are important, this may create some tensions and slow down investment, even though the available savings are globally sufficient. This may be more particularly so when the financial needs are not motivated by investments but by losses on current accounts.

As an 'ad hoc' criterion for our present purpose we may say that there is a risk of financial difficulties when either the variation of the nominal asset requirement M_f of firms or the variation of the ratio of M_f to the value of the physical capital stock, which is defined here as $P\bar{y}/\gamma$, is positive and high. In the first case the flow of funds required by firms is important; in the second case the solvency of firms is likely to be deteriorating (since no distinction is made between equities and bonds, one cannot be more precise and one cannot in particular necessarily associate a sustained high value of the ratio $\gamma M_f / P\bar{y}$ with lack of solvency or with financial difficulties).

We have seen that the full specification of the households' activity and of operations on goods and services suffices in our model to determine the evolution of real quantities and that some freedom then remains for the specification of some of the income and financial flows. Strictly speaking M_f is not fully determined in the evolutions that were studied. This remark stresses once more the fact that our examination of financial difficulties will remain sketchy here.

Restricting attention to the case in which the Walrasian stationary equilibrium is achieved with a zero rate of inflation $(\pi = 0)$, we are, however, in effect near to assuming that the net assets of the government sector are zero and therefore that M_f is equal to the assets M of households, which are fully determined in the evolutions considered here. Indeed, the equilibrium of financial operations and the budget equation of the government sector imply:

$$\dot{M}_f = \dot{M} - \dot{M}_g = \dot{M} - G + T \qquad (2)$$

whereas equation (22) of chapter 2 requires that $G = T$. Hence, $\dot{M}_f = \dot{M}$. Since we want to consider changes in M_f and $\gamma M_f / P\bar{y}$, we may equivalently examine changes in M and $\gamma M / P\bar{y}$.

Roughly speaking, these two proxies for financial tensions do not suggest that taking financial constraints into account would radically alter the conclusions derived in previous chapters. The first one $\dot{M}$, consumers' saving, is high when:

> output y is high,
>
> the real wage w is high,
>
> the real asset m is low,
>
> the rationing of consumers on the goods market is important.

Examination of $\dot{M}$ then suggests that financial constraints are unlikely in the Keynesian depression, whereas they may occur in the two cases in which consumption is rationed, i.e. in cases of inflation or of classical unemployment. But in these cases financial difficulties are more likely when the real wage rate w is high, i.e. when investment is also depressed by lack of profitability.

Looking for instance at the simulation that is presented in figure 3, we find that $M\,^{\cdot}$ increases up to $t = 10$ and then decreases. Its increase is particularly rapid at the beginning, being 2.5 to 3.5 per cent per period up to $t = 7$. But these are precisely the periods during which investment is negative, mainly because of lack of profitability. Since the financial constraints are likely to be more severe at the end of a period of rapid increase of M than at the beginning, we may guess that they delay somewhat the time at which investment will become positive again and hence perhaps also delay somewhat the turn from classical to Keynesian unemployment.

The second proxy varies as the ratio of consumer real wealth to productive capacity. In particular, it increases fast if real wealth increases fast and productive capacity decreases. Such a situation is not often found.

It occurs, however, in the simulation intended to mimic the impact of the oil shock. The initial situation was characterized by both a lack of profitability and a demand deficit; the latter was generated by assuming low real asset holding by consumers (600, instead of 900 in the Walrasian stationary equilibrium), which would not be all that realistic if an exact representation of the oil shock was claimed. Be that as it may, the simulation exhibits an increase of $\gamma M/P\bar{y}$ during the first nine periods, the cumulative increase amounting to some 22.5 per cent. These are precisely the periods during which investment is negative with first Keynesian and later classical unemployment. It may be that financial difficulties ought to be taken into account and would then delay the time at which investment becomes positive.

In the simulation of figure 3 the ratio $\gamma M/P\bar{y}$ decreases somewhat during the first seven periods because of the contraction of productive capacity; but the cumulative change amounts only to 5 per cent. It is difficult to infer any conclusion from such a limited shift.

Substitutability between capital and labour

In studying the role of profitability the present book has used a model in which the representation of technology is extremely simple: capital and labour are strictly complementary with absolutely no possibility of substitution between them. This extreme hypothesis certainly matters in the results that have been found.

In the medium run many possibilities of substitution are identified: some existing equipment can be operated with more or less labour, old and less productive equipment can be scrapped more or less early, new equipment can more or less economize labour at the cost of a varying degree of sophistication, the output mix can favour labour-intensive or capital-intensive products. The various choices among these possibilities depend on the economic evolution, both on its past and on its anticipated future; they depend in particular on the prices, wages, interest rates . . . Assuming an exogenously given capital intensity when the role of profitability in business fluctuations is studied therefore leads to a particularly crude theory.

Unfortunately, no simple model can be built that would correctly reflect the medium-term substitutability between capital and labour. The less complex one would probably be the now classical 'putty–clay' model, in which successive vintages of capital are identified and capital goods have a fixed length of life during which their mode of operation remains absolutely constant. At time t the capital stock is then made of A parts of various vintages: $v = t-1$, $t-2$, ..., $t-A$; the quantity of capital of vintage v is k_v (this is also the investment made in period v); its productive capacity if $\bar{y}_v$ and the productivity of the labour working with it is β_v (for all $t = v+1$, $v+2, \ldots, v+A$). But when equipment is built it may be made to be more or less capital intensive; in other words, neglecting technical progress, there is a function $f(\bar{y}_v, \beta_v)$ defining the amount of capital k_v that is required for building capacity $\bar{y}_v$ with labour productivity β_v (within some range of possible values for the latter). The function f is assumed differentiable and is increasing in both $\bar{y}_v$ and β_v.

Dealing with such a model would permit a much more complete and accurate representation of medium-term economic evolution than has been offered here. In particular the interest rate could be studied simultaneously with other components of the price system and it would be an essential component of the cost of capital. The theory would of course become quite complex.

However, as long as uncertainty about future prices and quantities is recognized, profitability will remain an important potential factor of investment behaviour, and consequently of unemployment. Indeed, it is likely to become a more important factor than with the fixed capital–output coefficient technology.

Consider for instance the investment decision in a situation in which the real wage rate is anticipated to be high. Then not only will the newly-built capacity be small relative to the expected demand, but also the new equipment will be designed to have a high labour productivity. The substitution of capital for labour will sustain investment and demand in the short run, but it will make classical unemployment deeper if such a situation holds. Even if Keynesian unemployment prevails, the short-run favourable impact is likely to lead later to higher unemployment, when the increase in labour productivity is felt.

If a bold guess is permitted, let us say that taking capital–labour substitutability into account would probably increase the sensitivity of economic evolution to changes in income distribution. Larger but also perhaps shorter fluctuations would probably result.

Index